JERSEY

OCCUPATION REMEMBERED

Compiled by
Sonia Hillsdon

Jarrold Colour Publications, Norwich

TO MY DEAR FATHER

Acknowledgements

Miss D. Vincent and Miss C. Jurd,
Public Reference Library, St. Helier
Miss M. de la Haye, La Société Jersiaise Library
Howard Butlin-Baker – for the original idea
Jack du Feu
Michael Ginns, C.I. Occupation Society
Michel Jeanne
Beth Lloyd, Radio Jersey
Richard Mayne
Mrs Gladys Whinnerah
Monty Doong

All those who shared their Occupation diaries and memories.

ISBN 0–7117–0252–7
© 1986 Sonia Hillsdon and Jarrold Colour Publications.
Published by Jarrold and Sons Ltd, Norwich. 186

CONTENTS

BIBLIOGRAPHY

Bailhache, V. J. *Heard in Jersey.* Bigwoods.

Baker, B. *Diary.* Unpublished. 1942–45.

Baker, H. B. *The German Occupation of Jersey 1940/45.* Reference Maps 1983.

Breadwinners (London) Limited. *German Military Underground Hospital,* Sanctuary Inns Ltd, c.1980.

Bullen, I. M. *Diary.* Unpublished. 1940–45.

Ed: Bryans, P. *Channel Islands Occupation Review.* C.I. Occupation Society. Various issues.

Croad, I. *Diary.* St. Columba's Church. 1940/45

Cruickshank, C. *The German Occupation of the Channel Islands.* Guernsey Press. 1975.

Evening Post. 1939/45.

Grandin, R. *Smiling Through.* Evening Post. 1946.

Man: Ed: W. L. Gerrard. *The Islander.* 1939/41.

Ed: Guillard, S. *Islander Magazine.* Channel Printers. Various issues.

Jeanne, M. *The Life of the Civilian Population of Jersey during the German Occupation 1940/45.* Unpublished thesis for Univ. Caen.

Ed: Rumfitt, M. *Jersey Evening Post.* Various issues.

Jersey Society in London. Bulletin, June and Oct. 1944.

Keane, M. *Hello, Is it All Over?* Ababuna. 1984.

Lloyd, Beth. *Programme series on Jersey's Occupation.* Radio Jersey. 1985.

Maugham, R.C.F. *Jersey Under the Jackboot.* W. H. Allen. 1946.

Mayne, R. *Channel Islands Occupied.* Jarrold 1978.

Mollet, R. *The German Occupation of Jersey 1940/45.* Société Jersiaise. 1954.

Ramsey, W. G. *The War in the Channel Islands Then and Now.* Battle of Britain Prints. 1981.

Sinel, L. *The German Occupation of Jersey.* La Haule Books. 1984.

States of Jersey. *Official Guide 1939.* States of Jersey. 1939.

States of Jersey. *Pamphlet. States of Jersey.* 1940.

Vaudin, M. *A Garland of Daisies.* Regency Press. 1984.

Williams, N. *Chronology of the Modern World 1763–1965.* Penguin. 1975.

Wood, A. & M. S. *Islands in Danger.* Four Square. 1965.

A Foretaste

The Second World War operations code named 'Green Arrow' and 'Nest Egg' began and ended a period that was unique in the history of the Channel Islands. 'Operation Grune Pfeile' (Green Arrow) was the German invasion in 1940 of those British islands in the English Channel which lie fifteen miles from France and a hundred miles from England. 'Operation Nest Egg' was their liberation by British Forces in 1945. So for nearly five years Jersey, Guernsey, Alderney and Sark were occupied by the Nazi forces of the Third Reich. These four islands – alone in Great Britain – came under the direct dictatorship of Adolf Hitler.

Yet no straight comparison can be made between the Occupation of the tiny Channel Islands and the vast territories in western Europe also occupied by the Nazis. In Jersey alone – with an area of a mere forty-five square miles and a population of only 40,000 – up to 11,500 German troops were garrisoned. In such a confined space and with approximately one German for every four Jerseymen, an underground resistance on the lines of the French Maquis was unthinkable.

Each one of the four Channel Islands also fared quite differently during the Occupation. Alderney was almost completely evacuated. The other three were affected by their proximity to England or France. Much too depended on whom the Islanders had at their head to negotiate the best terms for them with the German Commandant. Jersey is the largest of the Channel Isles, the nearest to France and during the Occupation was led by their Bailiff, Alexander Coutanche – a remarkable and decisive man.

Then just as no Guernseyman or Islander from Sark would have had a period of Occupation identical with a Jerseyman's, so even on the one island of Jersey experiences could be totally unalike. Where you lived – town or country, where you were employed, how rich you were, whether you were caught disobeying a German order – all made a difference as to how you fared in the Occupation. Some families grew rich on the illegal profits of the Black Market; others lost all they had. Some Islanders never had cause to speak to a German once in the nearly five years; others actually worked alongside the enemy.

And that was where the Occupation caused the greatest dissension in the close-knit community of Jersey. If a man worked with the Germans, was he just obeying Nazi orders or was he collaborating? If

Holidaymakers in Jersey prior to the Occupation

a woman reported a neighbour for defying a Nazi regulation, was she protecting the Island from wholesale reprisals or was she currying favour for her own ends?

Whatever the extenuating circumstances in individual cases, in the strictest sense of the words Jersey did undoubtedly have a small number of both collaborators and informers. What is more, as a direct result of information given, Jersey men and women died at the hands of the Germans.

Anyone, therefore, who looks back over the period of the Occupation is aware that, amidst the tales of horror and heroism and the hand to mouth daily existence, there were several sensitive areas. And these still rankle. So it is not surprising that among the many who are willing to share their Occupation experiences there are some who prefer to do so anonymously and without naming any names. Even after forty years, no one wants to stir up for those with long memories any unpleasantness from the past.

The following recollections come from those looking back forty years later and from the daily or weekly jottings of four Occupation diarists: Miss Izette Croad, Mrs Iris Bullen, Mr Bernard Baker and Mr Leslie Sinel. Both groups have built up a vivid picture of Jersey Occupation Remembered for which future generations who were not there will always be grateful.

At Last

BRITAIN DECLARES WAR ON GERMANY

Shock was the initial reaction of the Channel Islanders to the Occupation of their native islands. From the outbreak of war in September 1939 to the fall of France nine months later, they were fully convinced that their fate during hostilities would be identical to that of the rest of Great Britain: they would be defended up to the hilt and to the last man from all German attack by sea or air.

The natural identification of the Channel Islanders with the rest of His Majesty's British subjects on the mainland began from the day war broke out. When on Sunday, 3rd September 1939, the British and French finally declared war against Germany, Jersey's reaction, along with the other Channel Islands, was the same as that in England.

'At Last' was the headline in Jersey's *Evening Post* on Monday, 4th September. The paper reported that at sea the buoys and lighthouse lights had been extinguished at night as from the weekend; that on land Jersey's government, the States, in its *Use of Petrol* notice asked Islanders 'to refrain from using motor vehicles unnecessarily'.

Readers were informed on that first wartime Monday that the Channel Isles were to be included in the British Government's immediate scheme to limit foreign travel by the issue of permits. An Emergency Sitting of the States was reported as deciding that a permit would also be needed by any alien wishing to leave the Island. In one column was notice of the Parish by Parish distribution of gasmasks. In another the frank acknowledgement that in Jersey there were not actually enough gasmasks to go round!

On a lighter note, the cinema advertisements told their patrons that by order of the Bailiff, Jersey's Civil Leader, no films were to be shown that day, though West's Cinema and the Forum announced that their cafés would remain open. A special Jersey touch – dominated as the Island then was by its agricultural industry – was the following notice: 'Will all Farmers please co-operate in the Emergency Storage Scheme by sending to their Corn Merchants all the grain sacks they have available'. A scheme Islanders had cause to be thankful for in the isolated years to come.

The greatest impact of the War's outbreak, however, was seen in Jersey's capital down at St. Helier harbour. As early as 5.30 a.m. crowds of people had gathered on the pier. It was not only holi-

Coffee and tea supplies were still available in August 1940, as this illustration from *The Islander* depicts

daymakers queuing to return home, but also hundreds of French Reservists responding to their country's call after receiving their *ordres d'appel*.

The Recruiting Office in Green Street, St. Helier, had also been busy, 'inundated with applications and enquiries' and at times 'absolutely crowded out'. So in the long queue waiting for a boat, there were many Jerseymen ready to join up and serve their king.

For those left behind, the Evening Post carried many an advertisement to show that there was indeed a war on. Besco Laundry regretted 'that owing to several of our employees being called up for National Service our collection service is temporarily disorganised'. Jersey Motor Cycle and Light Car Club was 'being temporarily wound up owing to the present situation'. The paper also carried a reprimand to those who were alleged to be hoarding coal – 'five or six tons at a time'!

The prevailing mood of Islanders at that time was perhaps best summed up in the notice: 'War or no War our Mr F. N. Foster placed a stock order for over £1,000 worth of Pye receivers at the Radio Show last week and the new models are just arriving'. The people who bought those new models in 1939 could never have imagined their importance, less than a year later, to both Islanders and Germans. To the first they were a vital link with England, to the second a means of reprisal.

Therefore, for Islanders in September 1939 the war was only going to be a temporary interruption in normal Island life; while it lasted the interruption was going to cause as little disruption as possible. As *The Islander* magazine for that September put it: 'there were three days of this whirlwind activity and then once again things settled down'.

Jersey – Ideal Wartime Holiday Resort

So well indeed did life settle down in the months after war was declared, that Jersey's Tourism Committee felt confident that the Island had something special to offer to all those war-harrassed mainlanders in need of a holiday. In the spring of 1940 Tourism printed a pamphlet to reassure tentative tourists. Its front cover proclaimed 'Facts and General Information on Wartime Holidays in Jersey Channel Islands'.

Inside the pamphlet were the questions people on the mainland might·be asking themselves, together with the answers – in Jersey's favour! First and foremost was considered, 'Is it right to take

States pamphlet 1940 inviting tourists to Jersey

Food Control Office information showing the rations allowed by catering establishments

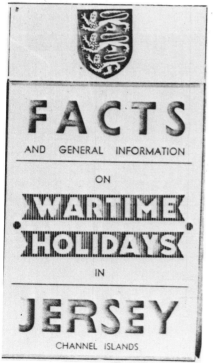

FACTS

AND GENERAL INFORMATION

ON

WARTIME HOLIDAYS

IN

JERSEY

CHANNEL ISLANDS

FOOD CONTROL OFFICE.
JERSEY.

THE ATTENTION OF THE PUBLIC IS DRAWN TO THE FACT, THAT CONSUMPTION OF SUGAR IN CATERING ESTAB- LISHMENTS IS RESTICTED TO ONE-TENTH OF AN OUNCE PER MEAL SERVED TO NON- RESIDENTS, PLUS A FURTHER AMOUNT OF ONE-TENTH OF AN OUNCE PER HOT BEVER- AGE SERVED.

A. LE GRESLEY.
Food Controller.

MAY, 1940.

9

Advertisement from the *Jersey Official Guide*, States Information Bureau, 1939

holidays in wartime?' and the reply came with all the safeguard of British Government approval:

'The official view is that money is well spent on annual holidays since the individual returns to his work refreshed mentally and physically and ready to give of his best in the interests of the national war effort.'

Once satisfied that it was morally alright to take a break from the war effort, the next poser for would-be-holiday makers was naturally 'Where shall we go?'. Again the answer came:

'JERSEY offers you an ideal solution to that problem. Situated as it is in the English Channel and sheltered by France, the geographical position of Jersey makes it the ideal resort for wartime holidays.

Happily our Island is far removed from the theatre of war. The bays with their eternal sands, sea and sunshine together produce an atmosphere of peaceful tranquillity strangely different from the rest of the world. Jersey offers you a haven for respose and recreation and it is in such calm surroundings that you will, at least temporarily, be able to banish the spectre of war from your mind.

The 'change' which you seek is to be found in Jersey – only radio and daily newspapers can remind you of the war.'

The next problems for Tourism to solve for visitors were, 'Do I have to get a permit? Are there restrictions? How can I get there?' Easily dealt with! 'No Travel Formalities Whatsoever Now Exist – You purchase your ticket precisely as pre-war, free from all restrictions.' Any other Restrictions? 'The restriction on the export of currency that was introduced at the commencement of the war was withdrawn on the 19th January 1940.' And as for food:

'Plans have been made to meet the demand likely to be caused by an influx of visitors during the summer months so please harbour no fears on that score. You will be allowed the same quantities of rationed foodstuffs as you obtain at home but to avoid unnecessary complications DO NOT FORGET TO TAKE YOUR CARDS ON HOLIDAY.'

The ways to get to Jersey in the first half of 1940 were the same as now, by plane or boat – only the names and fares were different. Jersey Airways maintained 'frequent services every day between Shoreham airport and the Channel Islands' – £5 Return and £3 Single, HM Forces being allowed a ten per cent concession. The Southern Railway had 'an excellent service of steamers' operating from Southampton to Jersey 'splendidly equipped to suit modern conditions,' Saloon and Third at £3.15.2 Return, 2nd Boat 3rd Rail at £2.13.3 Return.

From a free copy of the Official Guide from the States Information Bureau, visitors would be able to get information about hotels, holiday camps and boarding houses – 'You cannot go wrong if you

11

choose a hotel which advertises in that publication'.

To take just three hotels recommended in the 1939 Official Guide it is interesting to note what they offered the tourist in the summer of 1940. The Hotel Metropole claimed that it was the only hotel in St. Helier with 'extensive gardens of two acres – always a mass of bloom'. No question of digging that all up for Victory vegetables! Nor was there gloom at the Aberfeldy either, for 'life's just *grand* at Aberfeldy Hotel. You ought to be happy here. For 15 years we have been trying to anticipate your wishes. There is a First-class orchestra daily in the Dining Room, Dancing nightly with frequent Fancy Dress and Novelty Dances, Electrical Gymnasium, Tennis Court and Tournaments, A licence for Drinks and ample Lounge Accommodation for the 300-odd Holiday Makers invariably to be found here during the season. Aberfeldy's success is based on a reputation for good food. It is a reputation we intend to maintain'.

As for the 150-roomed Palace Hotel – it called itself 'The Premier of the Channel Islands' occupying 'the healthiest and most beautiful position in Jersey'. It boasted a 450-foot long Sun Terrace enjoying 'glorious and uninterrupted' views of St. Clement's Bay and rural St. Saviour.

Now, with hindsight, we can pinpoint the irony of Tourism's optimistic phrases, summed up by its slogan 'Jersey – Ideal Wartime Holiday Resort'. From Occupation records, it is also possible to note the very different summer season that befell the three hotels.

Certainly after June 1940 Jersey's proximity to France was no longer in its favour. Consequently 'Our Island' did not long remain 'far removed from the theatre of war'. Nor after 1st July 1940 were radio and daily newspapers the only reminder to Islanders of the war – there were the German Occupying forces themselves.

The hotels? The Metropole with its two acres of blooms was to become the Jersey Head Quarters of the German Army; the Aberfeldy was to be the Head Quarters of the German Engineer Battalion 319. The prestigious Palace Hotel – after serving as a Military Communications Centre and Officers' Training school – was to be blown up by the Germans 'in mysterious circumstances', just two months before the end of the war.

Waiting for a Miracle to Happen

The euphoria that could sustain the publicity of Jersey as the ideal wartime holiday resort was shattered before the Island's summer season could get into its stride. The *Evening Post* began to give details in the last weeks of May of the swift advance of German troops through Holland, Luxembourg and Belgium – an ever increasing threat to France and the British forces fighting there.

It next reported the Belgium surrender on 28th May 1940, when the 'felon' king Leopold, 'betrayed his country and broke his constitutional oath'. This meant that the British forces, fighting a rearguard action through capitulating France, had no choice but to make for the northern beaches. On 29th May their evacuation from Dunkirk began. Two days later the *Evening Post* editorial exhorted its readers with the one word 'Steady'.

On 4th June, the paper had given a welcome to the 'Boys from Jersey who are safely back from the Boulogne and Dunkirk fighting'. 'Hell, an experience I shall never forget,' according to Lance Corporal Brochet. But he praised the Navy and 'the fellows on all the auxiliary craft without whose help they would never have come through' – (many Jersey boats were amongst them).

With the German forces now so close to Jersey, no wonder that the *Evening Post*'s Headline on 5th June asked, 'What of the future?'. Many English residents had already begun to leave the Island before the last soldier had been rescued from the beaches of Dunkirk. Many Jerseymen, on the other hand, felt that an immediate plan to defend their Island should be put into operation. For the women to have formed a War Emergency Committee to make hospital requisites and for the men to attend Air Raid precaution lectures at the A.R.P. school at Fort Regent were not considered enough. Pentagram's letter to the *Evening Post* was typical:

'The urgent necessity for our Defence Committee is to re-constitute the Island Defence on the 1914 lines. To call up every able bodied man, irrespective of age and put them into their permanent defence works (trenches, Martello Towers, barbed wire entanglements and so forth) at once and let them carry on their work and their training under the supervision of the hundreds of old soldiers and sailors on this Island.'

Then came ten days of swift and contradictory events. As the retreat of the Allies from France began on 9th June – the smoke from the burning of their oil dumps could clearly be seen across the water – here in Jersey a defence plan did begin to take shape. About

13

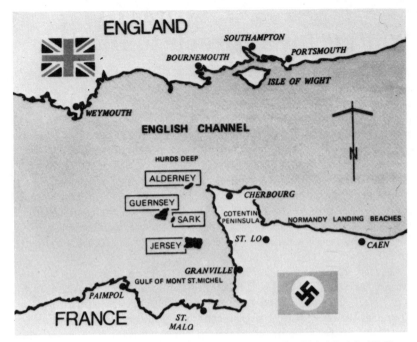

The military significance of the Channel Islands to the Third Reich (H. B. Baker)

1,500 men enrolled in the newly-formed Jersey Defence Volunteer Force. On the 15th June, British troops in their thousands, with ammunition and stores, arrived in Jersey. They were soon to be seen digging trenches and putting up defences. Some were busy mounting anti-aircraft guns in the People's Park at Westmount. But the day before their arrival the *Evening Post* had at last published the most feared but inevitable communique, 'Paris is now in German hands. The city was entered at 7 o'clock last evening'. This was Europe's 'Fateful Hour' and, as the paper put it, 'The time for a miracle to happen has arrived'.

His Majesty's Government's 'urgent consideration' materialised in the immediate summons to London on 16th June of representatives from Guernsey and Jersey. But the vital matter under discussion at that meeting was not defence. It was the probable demilitarisation of the Channel Isles – leaving them defenceless.

The news came on Monday, 17th June – 'FRANCE CEASES TO FIGHT'. So at an Urgency Sitting of the States, a Curfew Order was passed. No one was to be out after 9.00 p.m. There was also a Public Health Committee Announcement offering to those who wanted it: 'Evacuation of Women and Children from St. Helier'.

Much of the rest of the local news, however, mirrored the fact that, whatever the situation in war-torn Europe, in Jersey it was the potato season. Schools were to be closed, not just to give time for war tension to ease but also to allow secondary pupils, with so many men away in the Forces, to help harvest the potatoes. The crop was such a heavy one in 1940, that it was agreed that a whole cargo should be offered as a free gift to Britain.

However, as the digging continued, so did the disputes about the congestion caused in the streets and at the harbour of St. Helier by the farmers anxious to ship the glut out of the Island. The outgoing potatoes were taking up the space needed by the incoming British troops. So applause was given in the States when the Bailiff hinted darkly that he would not allow mayhem down at the harbour to continue for 'the Port of St. Helier was being used for business far more important than potatoes'.

A Grave Decision

The day after France's capitulation, Churchill's stirring words 'We shall fight on' were not only applauded but warmly echoed in Jersey. Then came the body blow. To their bewilderment, Jerseymen learnt that they were not to be included in that fight, for on that Wednesday, 19th June – under the banner headlines 'A Grave Decision' – came the words:

> 'A decision of the most vital importance to the Island was taken today by the British Cabinet and announced to the States of Jersey this afternoon by His Excellency the Lieutenant Governor. This Island is not to be defended: it is to be completely demilitarised and declared an undefended zone.'

The report concluded by asking readers to keep calm, obey the regulations and to carry on, as far as was possible, with business as normal. But immediately underneath, in heavy type, was the dread word 'EVACUATION'. The British Government were offering shipping facilities for the 'immediate voluntary evacuation of women and children'. There would be similar facilities 'for men between the ages of 20 and 33 who wish to join His Majesty's Forces'. Other men would only be evacuated if there was room left on the ships to take them.

For those wishing to be evacuated, the procedure was for names and addresses to be handed in at the special office at the Town Hall in St. Helier before 10.00 p.m. or between 6.00 and 10.00 a.m. the following morning, Thursday the 20th June. A further notice stated: 'Information will, in the case of women and children be required to be given as to whether arrangements have been or will be made privately for the accommodation and maintenance or whether accommodation and maintenance should be provided for them by the appropriate United Kingdom authorities'. The *Evening Post* noted the alteration of Curfew from 9.00 to 10.30 'to facilitate registration'. Air Raid Precaution lectures – at Fort Regent – were cancelled till further notice.

What would follow this demilitarisation and evacuation? As the Bailiff, Alexander Coutanche himself recalled, it was impossible to describe 'the horror with which Jersey received the news that we were going to be declared an open town and that we were not going to be defended'. The next fear was – Occupation.

Having heard, therefore, the terrifying sounds of the last ditch fighting in France, together with rumours of the atrocities committed by the advancing Germans, nearly half the Island's population decided to go. They had no intention of staying in a Nazi-occupied Jersey. The queue of those registering at the Town Hall in St. Helier – to make sure they got a place aboard any ship in order to get away – was up to six deep and extended as far as the Opera House, almost a quarter of a mile away. Some people stood in that queue for ten or more hours. From a population of about 50,000, over 23,000 names were eventually registered.

There were also anxious would-be-evacuees at the banks. They wanted to withdraw all their savings, so that they would have something behind them when they started their new life in England. But at such short notice, and despite the £300,000 which had been specially brought over from England, the banks could not stand such massive payouts. So it was hurriedly agreed that withdrawals would be limited to £25 per person.

Margaret Vaudin, who in her book *A Garland of Daisies* tells how she went that day to her father's bank to help 'steady the staff', also noted, 'I do not remember any hysteria but an awful lot of people fainted because of the long wait in the sunny June weather'.

Included too among those who wanted to leave Jersey were many post office clerks, but because luggage was restricted to only two suitcases each, the post offices were crowded with people wanting to send parcels of possessions to England, either for themselves or for relatives and friends. So those working on the counter in the General Post Office in Broad Street were urged to stay to the last minute, when a special boat would come to take them away.

As one counter clerk remembers, 'The Post Office was packed – we didn't even have a chance to look up between customers. We were getting so hot working at such speed that for the first time ever we were allowed to serve behind the counter with our jackets off. But the special boat we were promised never came!'

Another group of workers who wanted to go, and actually did, were some of the medical staff from the General Hospital in St. Helier. Mauyen Keane in her book *Hello, is it all over?* describes the panic the evacuation announcement caused in the hospital:

'Inside the hospital, doctors, nurses and porters were pushing here and there. All of Matron's staff seemed to be queuing up outside her office to pick up their diplomas or references. Others went straight over to the hotel to pack, not even bothering to do that. Everywhere we went we heard words like, "Go, go now, while you still can, no one will be safe!"'

Despite the panic and the horrific warnings, Mauyen Keane, an Irish nurse, decided to stay.

Miss Val Caton's memories of the evacuation are also vivid for, with her mother, she was one of those who did decide to go. She was just thirty at the time and on that Wednesday, June 19th, it was her day off from the hairdressing salon. She was walking with a friend and her baby through town to join her mother:

'On my way there a friend passed me in her car and stopped me. Did I know, she asked, that everybody's got to be evacuated? Though this dramatic news was not strictly accurate, when I joined mother at my friend's house, we all got round the table and urgently discussed what we should do. Our friends decided that they ought to go because they had three sons who would prefer to join up rather than be forced to work under the Germans. We also decided to go.

Then we went our own ways. Mother rushed home to get things ready while I went quickly to the Savings Bank to get some money out. But the queue was so long and I heard they were giving such a little money to each person, that I didn't think it was worth waiting.

The husband of my friend with the young baby went to the Pier to register for us all while we did the packing. It was the first time in my life that I saw my mother cry – at the thought of leaving her home.'

Miss Caton, her mother and their friends decided there was no point in trying to get away that night because of the long queues already down at the harbour. So they left the house early next morning, not forgetting to leave money on the kitchen table for the milkman. The house keys, together with more money that they owed to other tradespeople, they left with a neighbour. Down at the harbour they waited and waited – swelteringly hot.

'My mother and I were not only in our best clothes but I was wearing my fur coat and my mother my fur stole which I had persuaded her to put on!'

There they were in their Sunday best, Miss Caton proud of her new terracotta-coloured shoes and hat, when they learned that the boat they were to go to England on had just unloaded – it was a dirty coal boat!

'It took about 52 hours to get to Southampton and there was one sailor on board with a revolver – I wondered what use it would be against a German aircraft! The captain was an exceptionally kind man and allowed my mother, the oldest passenger on board, and the babies the use of his own cabin. So my friend and I spent that long journey to England sitting on the floor looking after all the babies.

Once at Southampton we seemed to be in for a tedious wait while our papers were being sorted out. Suddenly, the air raid sirens went. We were hurriedly rushed through customs, and mother and I wondered as we went for shelter – was this the safety that we'd left Jersey for?'

Remaining At Our Posts

On the same Thursday that Val Caton and her mother eventually sailed away from Jersey, three speeches were made which changed many people's minds. The speakers were the Bailiff, Jurat Dorey and Judge Pinel. The latter did not mince his words as he spoke to his fellow Islanders in the Royal Square. He told them that 'It grieved him to see Jersey men and women fleeing in panic from their native Island'.

At the window of the States Committee Rooms, the Bailiff stood on a chair so that the crowds below him in the Square could see that he had not gone. He said he heard that 'Rumours had gone around that there was to be a general pack up of the powers-that-be. As far as he was concerned he would never leave and his wife would remain by his side'. The moving conclusion to this reassurance was that he asked the crowd to say with him 'God Save the King'.

In the States, Jurat Dorey, speaking with deep emotion, told the house 'that morning he had been filled with disgust . . . he did not understand those of old Norman stock, who should be rooted in the soil, pressing to leave. We, who were always a calm steady people, who had jogged along in our own way loving our lands and our surroundings. He would like the House to express its utter contempt at what these people were doing'. (Applause.)

Some, encouraged by this stand, others for personal reasons, then changed their minds about going. Finally, of the 23,063 registered to evacuate, only about 6,500 actually went. Various were the excuses people gave for not in the end leaving Jersey. One man and his wife had definitely agreed to go, she was already in the long queue at the Town Hall to register, when he went up to her and said 'I'm not going to go'. And so neither of them went. Another man, a farmer, had even got as far as registering at the Town Hall to leave the next day, but when the next day came he found he couldn't bear to leave his animals.

A woman, who was then a teenager in St. Helier, recalls that her father had decided he'd stay behind with their two eldest brothers, while her mother took her, her sister and younger brother to England. As the children were packing their things, their mother kept on calling out, 'you cannot take all this stuff' but as soon as no one was looking, they popped their precious ornaments back into the suitcase.

'Then, we were all packed and ready to go, when my eldest brother on

19

The *Antiquity* left St Helier harbour on 20 June 1940 with over 200
evacuees on board

leave from the RAF walked in. He was horrified. He'd seen all the
evacuees in England with their names pinned on their coats being herded
into trains. He turned to my father. "You're not letting them go – they'll
be treated like cattle". And that was that!

My sister and I were very cross with my brother – we'd been so excited
at the thought of going. In those days you didn't travel as much as now
and there were all our school friends leaving, just as if they were going on
holiday. My sister and I complained and said "Now we'll never see
London". We kept our suitcases packed for about six weeks after – just in
case'.

Another family, with their possessions stuffed into pillow-cases
because there were no more suitcases to be had, after being down at
the harbour for three days, eventually had to trek back home. A
policeman told them there would be no more boats.

But the States were already having to deal with the havoc left in
the train of the first day's hurried evacuation. Mr Coutanche told the
House that 'He had been advised that farmers are turning their
cattle loose and had threatened to burn their crops . . . that he hoped
the Constables of the various Parishes would take the animals in
hand for the benefit of the farm as well as for the benefit of the
cattle'. As to the departure of those in States employ, 'his advice was
that no official should leave his post without the permission of his
superior officer'.

The most poignant statistic recorded as a result of Wednesday's
mass exodus of Islanders was that 'In the last 24 hours the staff of
the Animal Shelter have had to destroy 2,000 dogs and a very large
number of cats'.

Hold Fast

On Thursday, 20th June 1940, when the panic to evacuate was at its height, the *Evening Post* published a moral tale to stiffen the backbone of those who were left . 'A resident of Samarès walking on the lawn in front of his house last night picked up a bright object lying on the grass. It was a brass button and on the obverse side were the words "Hold Fast". We commend this advice to our readers.'

And 'hold fast' Islanders did – for just over a week. First they had to stand by while Defence plans were put into reverse. On that Thursday the British troops who had only been in Jersey for five days were suddenly given instructions to embark. By 10.00 a.m. they had all sailed away on SS *Malines*. The same day, on SS *Hodder*, the Royal Jersey Militia left, who, as a complete unit, were later to become the 11th Battallion of the Hampshire Regiment. The final move was for the States to disband the recently formed Defence Volunteers.

Jersey's Lieutenant Governor, General Harrison, was recalled to England to resume his career as a regular soldier. In his place the Bailiff, Alexander Coutanche, was sworn in – in accordance with the British Government's plan – as the Island's Civil Lieutenant Governor. A more discreet departure for England was that of Jersey's aliens – four Germans and twelve Italians, most of whom were waiters.

Already many wealthier Islanders had crowded to the airport to pay any money to get away by plane. There were others who were willing to risk the delay and pay their own fare to sail to England on the mail boat, which sailed to Southampton every Tuesday and Friday until the end of the month. But the British Government's 'free' (Jersey had to pay for it after the war!) official evacuation by boat of about 6,500 ended on that Friday afternoon.

Of these hectic days of departures one woman has two distinct memories:

'I saw the artillery being taken by the British soldiers from Elizabeth Castle and I can remember, when the evacuees had gone, the abandoned cars left all over the Weighbridge.'

There were amazing stories going the rounds, as 'Here and There' in the *Evening Post* reported: 'It is freely stated, for instance, that people have actually been giving away their houses, in other cases farms and large properties are alleged to have been sold for as little

21

as £5'. Added was the salutary reminder 'such contracts, of course, have no legal value'.

Then there was the one about the farmer who immediately gave his farm, cattle and stock to his manservant Jean and his wife Marie so that he could take himself off to England. The couple were delighted with their unexpected gift and shared their good fortune with their neighbours by asking them to help themselves to some of the items that they did not want. But once he got down to the harbour, the farmer decided he did not fancy leaving after all. Having got so far, however, he thought he might as well make a day of it in town. On his return to his farm, alas, the astonished Jean and Marie had to revert to being servants once more and the neighbours had to return all those 'presents' to their rightful owner!

Saturday in town was nearly the same as usual. Most of the shops had re-opened and deposits were being put into banks once more. Shoppers were told that there was plenty of food in the Island but that shopkeepers were not allowed to supply any articles of food in excess of their normal requirements.

In each of the Parishes, the Constables, empowered by the States, were beginning their doleful task of going into abandoned houses. This was to save any perishable food and to see to the welfare of any animals that had been left behind.

Everyone, in town or country, was asked not to use the telephone except for matters of extreme urgency, as there were not enough operators to cope with all the calls the crisis had provoked.

Thus it was that routine days came again to the Island, whose population had now dwindled to about 40,000 and many of whose houses, shops, cafés, pubs – even petrol stations, were empty or unattended. Yet everyone was waiting for something to happen.

By Wednesday, 26th June, the Weighbridge was once more the centre of most of the action. As usual there were the farmers, with their strings of lorries, horses and carts which stretched along the Esplanade, waiting with their loads of potatoes to ship. But further along the front were the men who had been detailed to take down the criss-cross of wires that had been put across St. Aubin's Road to prevent the landing of enemy aircraft. Indoors, in many a States office and in some private homes, any document that might give either information or offence to the Germans was being destroyed.

While many people were burying their valuables in the garden, Margaret Vaudin's bank manager father was concerned about the bonds and bullion still held by the five Jersey banks. All this wealth might, in the case of invasion, be seized by the enemy. Getting no satisfaction from London, he took matters into his own hands:

'My father sent for a lorry and a number of old potato sacks. Several million pounds worth of bullion and bonds were bundled into the sacks and whisked off, accompanied by two of my father's clerks. I heard afterwards that their troubles only began when they reached Weymouth. Nobody would believe them and they had the greatest difficulty persuading anyone to help them. One man sat on the piles of sacks on the quay, whilst the other struggled with authority from a public phone box.'

Finally, on Thursday 27th, 'Here and There' noted in its column:

'Jersey Swimming Club at Havre des Pas appears to be making an attempt at "business as usual": deck chairs are laid out on the terrace. What a difference to this time last year!'

On that fateful day of demilitarisation, Jersey's Bailiff, Alexander Coutanche, had promised Islanders that they could sleep peaceably in their beds while the Union Jack still flew on top of Fort Regent. So, for the nine days following this 'grave decision', the Islanders did just that, though they were now defenceless and had little idea of what lay in store for them. Their peace was shortlived. The flag was only to be hoisted a few more times before being pulled down and then hidden away for almost five years.

Low flying German planes had been heard; their white trails in the summer sky had been seen. But nothing prepared Jersey for what was to happen on the evening of Friday 28th June.

Fierce Air Raids

As the *Evening Post* banner headlined the news next day:

'FIERCE AIR RAIDS ON CHANNEL ISLANDS. HARBOURS BOMBED. HEAVY CASUALTIES IN BOTH ISLANDS.

Nine people are known to have been killed and many injured in a bombing and machine gunning attack carried out by at least three and perhaps more German aircraft over Jersey last night.

The Harbour was the chief objective apparently and a bomb struck the pier, others fell in the Mulcaster Street and Commercial Buildings areas causing considerable damage to property belonging solely to civilians . . ..

One bomb at La Rocque fell harmlessly in the harbour and stuck in the mud, the other fell on the Gorey side of the shipway and it was this which caused the casualties.'

These are some of the reactions of those caught up in this attack which *The Times* condemned as 'barbaric':

'I happened to be standing on the verandah of the house at Westmount looking out, when, to my surprise, I heard some loud thumps towards the east of the Island and I thought "What on earth is that?" A few seconds later I knew, because I suddenly saw three planes coming across from the eastern side of the Island and I could see sort of silvery things dropping from then and then suddenly the explosions. I rushed in and said, "We're being bombed. Come on, let's get down stairs". '

Friday, 28th June, 1940 'During the morning one or two planes kept flying over us, so high up that we could not distinguish them, while some left their traces of smoke out. That afternoon we went with the children to Samarès. As we got off the bus we could still see planes very high up, some people said they were German and that they had been flying lower over the Pier, where they were busy loading potatoes in the boats for England.

I had started watering at the bottom of the garden when I heard planes over me. I looked up and saw three at a height where I could have distinguished them. I was standing there having a good look at them and trying to see the markings, when out of one I saw an object drop, a trace of smoke and then what seemed to be gunfiring. It was then that I saw I was in danger and as I was a little way off from home I stood upright against the hut till mother called me indoors.

The damage caused by the bomb which fell at the top of the slip at La Rocque Harbour facing Harbour View was considerable. The dead were Mr Adams who was killed at his door. Mr Pilkington, who lived at Mrs Dobbins, and Mrs Fanell who lived at Harbour View – they were all in the road at the time of the explosion. Uncle Frank had narrow escape. He was sitting on the seat which is situated on one side of the slip, and when he saw the danger he had the presence of mind to lay flat under the form, he also pushed a Miss Vellemont and two young children who were on the seat with him, and so they escaped being killed as they had been screened

Bomb damage at La Roque slipway

from the debris by the seat over them and the wall nearby. The people of the neighbourhood were all terrified, many of them ran into a nearby field and were crouched down in the ditches for safety.

Some cousins together in their La Rocque bungalow heard the explosion and one of them went out to see what had happened. But when she found that people had died, she soon came home.'

In the Post Office in Broad Street, a worker was on counter duty just before closing. 'When we heard the first bomb we dashed out into Commercial Street and were going towards Conway Street when another bomb fell – near the Pomme d'Or Hotel. We were both blown back with the blast. So we turned round and made for the Post Office again. People from shops nearby had by then run into the Post Office for shelter and we all huddled together in the passageway at the front of the stairs.'

Many of those living in St. Helier, fearing another raid, decided they would be safer staying with relatives or friends in one of the country parishes. One family, who lived near the Weighbridge and had seen the Esplanade as if it was on fire after the bomb on the harbour, almost immediately had a phone call from a farmer in Trinity inviting them to stay with him.

'We all got into the car, adults and children, and drove up to his farm where we were warmly told to come in. We slept in four poster beds and stayed there a fortnight.'

The air raid sirens did go again – twice on the Saturday morning. But no more bombs were dropped. In town, 'Shoppers spoke in glowing terms of the kindness and courtesy they received this morning in the air raid shelters provided by the business establishments'.

One shop assistant in Woolworth's who remembers exactly how she put her A.R.P. lessons into practice on that Saturday is Miss Hilda Marrett:

'The boss called me and told me to instruct the young ladies to put out the fire buckets. Then I was to tell the customers they might go home if they wished. Those remaining I had to tell to sit on the floor with their backs to the counters. If there were any children I could lend them toys from the toy counter to play with. This done I then went to turn off the gas and the electricity. So all I could offer the customers was a drink of water. There was one poor old lady crying, "They machine gunned me all down my garden path at La Rocque last night".'

Why did *The Times* call the German air raids on Guernsey and Jersey, with their total of thirty-three 'murdered' civilians, 'barbaric'? It did so because they thought that the Germans, from as early as June 21st, had known that the Channel Isles had been declared a demilitarised area. This, however, was not the case. Not even the British public knew that. They learned about the withdrawal of troops and the Islands being undefended for the first time on the very day of the bombing. The news was broadcast that evening by the BBC.

But this was still not a direct statement to the German government declaring St. Peter Port and St. Helier 'Open Towns'. Only on Sunday, 30th June, was a message given to the Germans themselves – via the United States Embassy in Berlin: 'The evacuation of all military personnel and equipment from the Channel Islands was completed some days ago. The Islands are therefore demilitarised and cannot be considered in any way as a legitimate target for bombardment'.

Why such procrastination on the part of His Majesty's government? It was feared that an avowal that the Channel Isles were no longer defended would be tantamount to giving the Germans an open invitation to invade them. It was – and the next day they did.

Hauling down the Jack

At 5.30 in the morning of Monday 1st July, a message was dropped at the airport by a German plane. It was addressed to the Chief of the Military and Civil Authorities and called on the Island to surrender. It was taken straight to the Bailiff. A farmer up early to milk his cows heard the sound of an engine. 'I looked up and lo and behold a plane with the Swastikas on. I thought to myself, they've arrived this time.'

But the parachuted message in the container, (two others were also dropped) was only the herald of the Germans arriving. The details of the ultimatum given by General Richthofen (German Commander of the Air Forces in Normandy) to the Bailiff were that to signify the Island's willingness to surrender, three large crosses were to be painted in prominent places and white flags were to be hung out of every building. A peaceful surrender, it went on, would ensure the safety of the life, property and liberty of all the Islanders. But if these signs of a peaceful surrender were not in evidence by 7 a.m. the next day, 2nd July, then the Island would be heavily bombarded.

Before that, though, at 11 o'clock, another German plane approached the airport. This time it landed and a German Air Force officer assured the airport authorities in perfect English, 'I don't want any trouble. I want to speak to the Bailiff'. Lieutenant Kern's purpose was to make sure that the Bailiff had received the ultimatum and to tell him that the Occupying Forces would start to arrive that very afternoon.

In fact, copies of the ultimatum had already been put up, with an extra notice ordering Islanders to offer no resistance whatsoever to the occupation of their Island. So after hearing the message phoned from the airport, that a young Luftwaffe officer wanted to see him, Coutanche first spoke to crowds of people crammed into the Royal Square, wondering what was happening.

After he had read the ultimatum to them, he explained that the Islanders, undefended as they were, had no choice but to surrender. Coutanche then told everyone to keep calm, to obey the orders the Germans gave and to go home and make sure that every building flew a white flag.

Various are the memories of all those fluttering white flags which preceded the entry of the first Germans into St. Helier. Those flying from the airport poles were torn up pillow cases: a mother in

To the Chief of the Military & Civil Authorities
(Jersey, St. Helier)

1. I intend to neutralize military establishments in Jersey by occupation.

2. As evidence that the Island will surrender the military and other establishments without resistance and without destroying them, a large white cross is to be shown as follows, from 6 a.m. 2nd July, 1940.

   (a) In the centre of the Airport in the East of the Island (A mistake, this was really the Royal Jersey Golf Course.)

   (b) On the highest point of the fortifications of the Port.

   (c) On the square to the North of the Inner Basin of the Harbour. Moreover, all fortifications, buildings, establishments and houses are to show the White Flag.

3. If these signs of peaceful surrender are not observed by 7 a.m., July 2nd, a heavy bombardment will take place.

   (a) Against all military objects.
   (b) Against all establishments and objects useful for defence.

4. The signs of surrender must remain up to the time of the occupation of the Island by the German troops.

5. Representatives of the Authorities must stay at the Airport until the occupation.

6. All Radio traffic and other communications with Authorities outside the Island will be considered hostile actions and will be followed by bombardment.

7. Every hostile action against my representative will be followed by bombardment.

8. In case of peaceful surrender, the lives, property and liberty of peaceful inhabitants are solemnly guaranteed.

The Commander of the German Air Forces in Normandy,
Richthofen, General.

The German Ultimatum

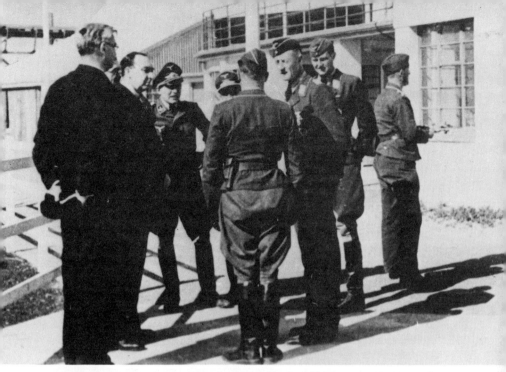

The Bailiff and the Attorney General meet the first Germans on Jersey soil at the airport

Belmont Road hung out one of her baby's nappies: some white knickers, holey vests and underpants were put out to register disgust. One woman, having seen to her house in St. Helier, rushed off to hang a piece of white material outside the family's summer home at La Rocque. She feared, as many did, that something terrible would happen to those buildings without their white badge of surrender.

'The most tragic time of the day was when we were all informed that we all had to have a white flag of surrender flying from every house in the Island by 7 a.m. on the Tuesday morning, the time when the Germans were to occupy the island. So we were all busy making and erecting this unhappy flag.'

Someone in town remembers that the whole of King Street was a mass of white flags. Margaret Vaudin expresses her memory of them thus:

'I shall never forget the sight of those white flags hanging from every house. It was both sickening and demoralising, and I never felt more depressed in my life.'

Left: The White Cross in the Royal Square

Once Coutanche was told that the Germans had actually landed at the airport, he realised that his assurance to Islanders that 'they could sleep peaceably in their beds so long as the Union Jack flew on top of Fort Regent' no longer held good. It was time 'to go and haul down the Jack'. Then he, as both Lieutenant-Governor and Bailiff, and Duret Aubin, the Attorney General, drove to the airport to meet the first Germans on Jersey soil.

From the airport the two Jerseymen were accompanied by the Germans on their way back to St. Helier. Once the Germans had checked in the Post Office that the telephone cables with England had been cut, they made the Town Hall their Military Headquarters. One of the crowd of people outside the Town Hall at that time, waiting around for someone to tell them what to do, recalls suddenly seeing a flag being hauled up above their heads. It was the first Swastika to be seen in Jersey.

The panic that many householders felt on that first day of Occupation is mirrored in the fears of one St. Helier family. They fully expected the Germans to come immediately and search every house, taking away with them anything they fancied. So they decided to hide as much of their food and their drinks as they could:

'We had a trap door in the roof of our scullery, so I stood on the top of the step ladders while the rest of the family passed me all the food they could find. Once the food was up there the trap door was so narrow and it was such a business to get at it that we thought twice about bringing it out. Later it was quite exciting bringing the food out bit by bit – "ooh look at this" we used to say – and in fact what we had hidden lasted most of the first year. The drink we buried in the yard and we used to dig up a bottle of whisky for special occasions such as Christmas. Once we thought we had lost two of the bottles! But there wasn't really any need to do what we did – the Germans didn't search every house as we thought they would.'

First Impressions

'I was going for a walk with my two children along Mont au Prêtre when a big German on a motor bike passed me. He got off to put a notice on the stone wall saying that German troops would be arriving the next day and then off he roared.'

'The first intimation I had of what was going on was when I was returning home, coming along near Rouge Bouillon. I was just driving the car normally when to my astonishment about 40 or 50 German soldiers suddenly appeared on bicycles – riding on the wrong side of the road! So I pulled to one side and looked at these chaps going by and thought, "What on earth's going on here? Where have they sprung from?".'

'So there was me basking on the top of the wall at West Park in my khaki shorts when I heard them, singing at the tops of their voices as they marched along St. Aubin's Road going towards St. Helier.'

'I went down into the town and to my surprise I found outside the Town Hall a German soldier with a rifle over his shoulder, on guard, and outside the Post Office another one and I realised then that our communications with Britain had been cut. We were suddenly isolated from all contacts which were of value to us. Indeed, suddenly one realised that our home had become our prison.'

'I was walking down to town with my mother and when a group passed us they wouldn't step off the pavement. When we got home my mother told Dad in great indignation, "When we met some Germans in town we had to step off the pavement into the road".'

'There were great swarms of soldiers in the shops buying up as fast as they could. They couldn't get things like that in Germany. They were even buying presents for their wives and girl friends.'

'The manager of Woolworths told all the young ladies to go to their places behind the counters and then he said: "I am going to open the doors and the Germans will come in. You must obey my instructions. Whatever a German asks for you give him but don't ask for money. Let them take whatever they like." When the doors were opened they thronged all over the place.'

'After that first two weeks there was nothing left in town.'

'When I went to Beghins for a pair of lady's shoes all they had left in the shop were two pairs of men's sandals, Clark's size 7. I bought a pair and they lasted me the whole Occupation.'

'I remember there was an ice-cream vendor in Roseville street and the German soldiers gathered round buying ice-creams. They wanted to give some to a few local children who were watching these strange soldiers but the children were reluctant to accept anything from the men in German uniform.'

'The Luftwaffe Officers spoke with an Oxford accent. They would come into the Post Office and say "I would like one each of your stamps, please". These were for their stamp collections; they had their own field Post Office in Beresford Street.'

'I heard one German say to another that he was going to motor cycle to Guernsey.'

'Some Germans were overheard boasting in a shop "One more week and we'll be in London". '

'A friend told me that one of the assistants at de Grunchy's had told him that a German had been in to get an evening suit to wear in London next month!'

'I found all the traffic suddenly being on the right very confusing.'

'That first night at 2 a.m. I heard the sound of soldiers marching up Beach Road. I broke out into a sweat of fear and got back into bed again soaking wet.'

'There were the Germans basking in the sun at the front of the Grand Hotel.'

Tuesday, 2nd July 'Went to Church Work Party in afternoon for a last meeting – we had been busy making gloves for Mine Sweepers and so tidied up and put everything away. On the way up saw two sights which struck me as comical:

First, an old-fashioned calico chemise attached to a stick serving as a white flag.

Second, ten or twelve of the invaders on the steps of the Royal Hotel, no rifles, tin hats, gas masks etc., but bathing attire neatly rolled under their arms with car at door to take them to disport themselves on the beach. Was told there were crowds of them at the Havre de Pas Bathing Pool. A rope stretched across another street bore a pair of Victorian long-legged calico drawers floating in the breeze.'

Goosestepping along the Parade in St Helier

A German soldier and one of St Helier's policemen outside the Town Hall –
'Rathaus' to the Germans, 'Rathouse' to the locals!

'I was surprised to find that they looked like any young people, how well
built they were, how English they looked.'

'They looked very handsome in their great capes, that first lot.'

'I saw them in town that first or second evening, bivouacked around the
Cenotaph with their rifles propped up one against the other. That very
evening girls were going out with them.'

'In the Parade I saw a whole host of German soldiers standing around
listlessly, looking somewhat bemused, with all their equipment and
children running round and being given sweets and so on, and I thought
"Really, where is the slaughter? Where is the butchery?"'

It'll all be over by Christmas

The Occupation was not followed by instant barbed wire and bunkers. Why not? Because the Germans saw the Channel Isles as a mere stepping stone to England. Some soldiers even thought they were in the Isle of Wight and it was only a matter of purchasing a train ticket for London! After their swift conquest of Europe, the Germans were convinced they were going to win the war, and soon. In fact Coutanche was told by the Germans what a lovely island they would make of Jersey after it was all over.

Three weeks after the invasion, the *Evening Post* was ordered to publish a daily edition for the troops to be called *Deutsche Inselzeitung* with its front page in German. The editor, Dr Kindt, claimed that this would be the first German newspaper printed in the British Empire – 'for the moment'. The Nazi boasted that the war would be over in three weeks, because taking England would be 'just a manoêuvre'.

The German title of the *Evening Post*

So, in preparation for the invasion of England the Germans started their bombing attacks. First it was Channel shipping, then ports and RAF aerodromes. Finally the target was London. The British response to this blitz in the late summer and autumn of 1940 was the Battle of Britain.

Meanwhile in Jersey the German troops settled in under Haptmann Gussek. An occupying force numbering about 1,750 to control just forty five square miles. Within a year the numbers were to increase to 11,500. The Jersey response was to continue to live as normally as possible.

The *Islander* magazine in its first Occupation issue captures both the humour and the determination to carry on that was true of the majority of Islanders in those first six months of living under German bureaucratic rule. Its editorial in July 1940 begins: 'The *Islander* is still with you. It has not been evacuated – nor has it been

"lodged au greffe" – nor has it been rationed.'
In the autumn came the added fillip of the news sheets dropped in the Channel Islands by the RAF.

Tuesday, 24th Sept. 'Great excitement to-day, news sheet apparently dropped by RAF found at St. Ouen.'

Wednesday, 25th Sept. 'Have seen the news sheet to-day about 12 inches by 10 inches, Headed *English News* and underneath with No. 1 Sept. 1940. Firstly the King's message. "The Queen and I desire to convey to you our heartfelt sympathy in the trials which you are now enduring. We earnestly pray for your speedy liberation knowing that it will surely come." '

But there was to be no 'speedy liberation'. It was not all over by Christmas and the 'Editor's. Window' in the *Islander* of December 1940 looks out onto an Island swept by rumour and restricted by rationing as he extends Christmas greetings and wishes Happy New Year to his readers.

'Both international and local events have brought to the fore that interesting but odious specimen, the gossip and scandalmonger. No Act can be passed without a comment, which is always far-fetched, rash and frequently imbecile, made up of general reflections containing no thought and scarcely a phrase that has not been overworked. His ears are long and his eyes are quick, but especially so with regard to perceiving faults which are more often than not increased by intermeddling. Rumours sweep through the town and country-side with an amazing rapidity and cause many nervous or highly strung people quite unnecessary fears, anticipations and worry. We think that this form of amusement should cease.

The dark, long, winter nights are approaching and, the black-out and curfew tending to anchor people to the fireside, there are in this particular, two main commodities which will be required: fuel for the fire and fuel for the mind. We hope that the States' Schemes of peat cutting and wood felling and also the import of coal and coke will be sufficient to satisfy the demand in the first case while the Public Library will no doubt do its best to satisfy most people in search of reading matter. Owing to the limited size of the fiction section, habitual novel readers would be well advised to realise that biographies and books of travel can be just as entertaining. To this end, we propose, in next month's issue of the *Islander*, to give short reviews of some non-fiction books obtainable at the Public Library which might be of interest to readers.

With the limited resources at one's disposal, it is only the expert cook who can concoct a tasty dish. For those devoid of the "culinary art", we strongly recommend the daily Communal Meal served at the Technical School in Phillips Street. Here a splendid hot meal of soup and meat or vegetable dish may be obtained for 6d. For an additional 1d. or 2d. a dessert of some kind is served. We understand that many of the vegetables used at the Communal Kitchen are obtained from the products of the Stadium Scheme mentioned in last month's *Islander*. The Communal

STATES OF JERSEY.

St. Helier's Community Restaurant

will be opened on TUESDAY, OCT. 22nd,

In the St. Helier House Hotel Dining Room

(ENTRANCE IN HILARY STREET).

Mid-day Dinner will be served from 12.30 to 2 p.m.,
consisting of Soup, Meat and/or Vegetable Course.
Sweet. **At an inclusive price of 1/-.**

SEPARATE TABLES FOR FOUR.

MEAT COUPONS WILL NOT BE REQUIRED.

One of the communal eating places which helped Jersey people to eke out their Occupation rations

meals are planned by Miss Fraser, who is the cooking instructress at the School, while the efficient service is performed by an enthusiastic body of voluntary helpers, who together with Miss Fraser, deserve all praise. If we make one small criticism, it is that there seems to be somebody entrusted with the seasoning who is inordinately fond of pepper and peppers on the same principle as the Duchess in *Alice in Wonderland* who said "he can thoroughly enjoy pepper when he pleases".

It is with great pleasure that we learn that the sugar ration for children has been increased to 8 ounces per week. In these times, when attention is concentrated on the war, we ought to be extremely thankful to the authorities concerned for having had such foresight with regard to the generations who will, we hope, inhabit a more peaceful and prosperous world.

This attention to the health of children brings us to another aspect: their education. Many boys and girls who would normally have left school and obtained employment are now kicking their heels at home, there being as it is, a surplus of both skilled and unskilled workers in the labour market. Might not this be an opportunity of extending the school leaving age, thus equipping the man and woman of the future with an education which will be a real use to them in playing their parts as citizens?'

Restrictions

There had been wartime restrictions before the Germans invaded – blackout and the forbidden unnecessary use of motor vehicles were just two. There had been a curfew as France fell in June 1940. There had also been rationing, as there was in the rest of the British Isles. But these restrictions were as nothing compared with what the population of Jersey had to endure before they were liberated in May 1945. As Sinel records in his Occupation Diary on 31st October 1940:

'There is a new Order published almost everyday. These were put out by the German Commandant from his H.Q. at College House, Victoria College – "in close touch with Civil Authorities" – to whom even States Statutes had to be submitted. They were all "to be strictly obeyed".'

These Orders started from the first full day of the Occupation, 2nd July 1940, and continued to the very eve of the Liberation of Jersey. One of the last that was put out, on 5th May 1945, prohibited the sale of Union Jacks and other victory emblems. Many, because Jersey came under the regulations governing Occupied France, seemed quite unrealistic – allowing no-one within ten kilometres of coastal areas for example, did not allow much room for living on an island only nine miles by five!

'We have yellow notices plastered up all over the place printed in German and French, apparently what is posted up in Occupied France.'

Amongst the first orders to be issued were the prohibition of spirits – 'home-made cider became very popular at parties' – and the use of cars for private purposes – 'all cycle shops are sold out'. Most private and commercial vehicles were eventually commandeered by the Germans for their own use. Many were immediately taken out of the Island.

Friday, 26th July. 'On Thursday they had come to fetch Mr. Pirouet's (car) from Keppel Tower, a lovely green racing car of which the owner who is serving his country was very proud. It was shipped that evening.'

'Lord Haw Haw has broadcast the news that the Jersey people had been very kind to the Germans and were giving up their cars to help their German war effort!!'

'We are living through a curious phase just now, where once a car was commonplace; we now strain our necks just to catch a glimpse of such pre-historic vehicles as cabs, donkey-carts and traps, not to mention the peculiar contraptions one sees suspended from the backs of bicycles.'

'The weirdest trailer yet seen: an ordinary cabin trunk fitted with two wheels and towed behind a cycle gaily whistling along New Street.'

To make the Island fit into a Germanic scheme of things, all clocks and watches had to be put forward to Central European time and all traffic was switched from the British left of the road to the continental right. Reichsmarks were immediately substituted for sterling, seven to each £1 but could not be spent in Germany itself, where Deutschmarks were the only legal currency.

More irksome was the marking out of certain areas as 'Verboten' Military Zones and the necessity for everyone over 14 to carry an identity card, complete with photograph ('what photographs!').

'There were some amusing replies to the queries put on the Identity forms. One person put down for physical peculiarities, "Rheumatism".'

Then, though its timing varied, there was the ever relentless curfew.

'The beaches were out of bounds unless you were a fisherman.'

'We were supposed to tell if we slept out of our own homes. But we often went to our bungalow at La Roque for weekends. We used to go sandeeling'.

'We went for a cycle into the country and it got so late that we decided to stay away for the night. I telephoned the people across the road to tell my parents. But though they didn't say "no", it was after Curfew and they wouldn't take the risk of crossing the road. We enjoyed ourselves but my parents were worried the whole night through.'

'You weren't allowed to keep more than one dog but my friend had two, so she asked if she could register one in my name. One day she saw some German policemen and thought they were after her dogs. Much to my surprise she opened my door and threw one of the dogs into my house. "This one's yours," she said. "They're around." '

There were further incursions into personal freedom. Some people's very homes were taken from them – requisitioned. Many large

Soldiers of the cycle squadron outside requisitioned Brabant House in Trinity

The Horse comes into its "own" again.

Petrol difficulties solved again in Jersey,
as illustrated by our artist Miss M. Corrin.

Cartoon from *The Islander*, September 1940

houses, hotels, schools and guest houses had been taken over by the Germans from the very beginning but when in October 1941 even more troops were landed, including members of the youthful Reichsarbeitsdeinst – a para-military German labour corps, bringing the total up to nearly ten thousand, more homes went. It was a case of 'tenants again being turned out at very short notice and some told to leave certain articles of furniture behind'.

'The Park Estate and Tabor Estate at St. Brelade are practically entirely peopled by the Germans.'

'Things turned worse for us later on, because what had been a surprise for us that no one had come to take the house at Westmount ended eventually. Some very important officers turned up and said they were going to commandeer the house, so we would have to remove all the furniture. So after two years in that house we moved back into town.'

But the Order which affected all Islanders and which bit hardest was issued in June 1942. As Leslie Sinel records on 8th June:

'What we have dreaded for a long time has come to pass – all wireless sets belonging to the civilian population are to be handed in and retained in custody by the Feldkommandandtur; infractions of this order are punishable by imprisonment up to six weeks and a fine of 30,000 Reichsmarks (over £3,000)'.

'We had a battery set which had no batteries, so we were quite happy to hand that in. But that very day I took it in, I went to see a friend of mine who had been a wireless dealer, until his business folded up with the Occupation, and got him to make a little 2 valve set which operated some earphones, and I was able to retain this right through the war – at some considerable risk. My wife was very frightened about the whole thing but we kept the wireless in a biscuit tin covered over with some macaroni, while we had some macaroni, but eventually the time came when there wasn't any, so then we had to hide it under the sawdust fire.'

'We have always plenty of company listening to the news as there are no dry batteries to be had for a long while now. People cannot use their sets unless on the mains though some have had an arrangement which takes the place of a battery made from a number of jam jars filled with ammonia tablets in water. As these are very few and without mains around here I have welcomed all those who are eager to have news of our dear country which our hearts go out to even more now than ever before, to come in and listen to the news though it is really forbidden to congregate.'

'We kept our wireless and hid it up the chimney. The blacksmith made a couple of arms to keep it in place. All the neighbours used to come round

Germans interrupt a family scene (Jersey Museum exhibition, May 1985)

to listen. One night we were all sat there in a circle listening to the news, when there was a banging on the door. My brother went to see who it was. "Who the hell is it?" I asked. "Bloody Germans". So we put a record on our gramophone with a very old rusty needle. The sound was terrible. "Schöne Musik" said the German, as he saw everyone sitting round the gramophone.'

'We were living in a small cottage in Roseville Street which backed on to a nursery. Very near at hand were a lot of Germans. One evening we had our crystal set going and our head phones on to listen to it when there was a great knocking at the door. We hurriedly put the set away, pushed our headphones under the cushions and sat on them. My husband went to the door. He came back and said "There's a *greenfly* at the door and he wants to know if he could have some flowers because he's offended the cook and wants to apologise by giving him a bunch of flowers".'

'We used to rob telephone boxes of receivers in the middle of the night to make head pieces for crystal sets.'

'We put our head piece over an empty bucket and that amplified the sound.'

'To run our wireless set we had to use the car batteries which I was able to get my friend to charge up – we had these batteries in the house. Had the Germans come to search, of course, they would have been a source of suspicion. But we had an answer for that. We had got a piece of wire running up the wall and across the ceiling from which was suspended a very small bulb and the story would have been that that was what the batteries were for. In point of fact they were there to run our wireless set and I used to connect them up and walk around with a long lead listening to the BBC. And it was rather a strange thing for me to listen to the broadcasts and to see the thing from two points of view. In the days when the Germans were advancing into Russia and making tremendous strides – they in our local paper would claim all sorts of things which were not denied by the BBC but which were not reported. One would never hear of the Germans' advances till four or five days later. But when the tide was turned and the Germans were being pushed back in all directions, it was remarkable that in the local paper things would not appear until they'd been claimed four or five days earlier by the BBC!'

'You had to be careful after you'd been listening to the wireless that you weren't caught whistling the latest tunes you weren't supposed to know.'

'An employee from the Water Works used to bring us the news on his bike. He would hand us rice paper and on it, with no spaces, would be typed all the latest news. The idea was that once the news had been read you could eat the rice paper.'

'It wasn't only the BBC that was listened to. Radio Berlin could also be picked up and Lord Haw Haw, who had defected to the Germans, would speak after the news. Often he would give the names and prison of half a dozen prisoners of war held in Germany. Now the last we'd heard of my young brother was that he was lying ill on the field of battle. We didn't

Listening to a crystal set for the latest forbidden news of the war. (Jersey Museum exhibition, May 1985)

know whether he'd been taken a prisoner of war. Two years later a friend rushed in to say "I've heard your brother's name on Lord Haw Haw's programme after the news. He gave the Stalag number".'

'A trial of some 16 people was concluded early this week who were accused of receiving news by radio and talking about it. It appears that Mrs B. kept back one of her radio sets and buried it when the confiscation order came out. Later she gave permission to somebody living near to dig it out and use it. This person was apparently apprehended by the Gestapo about a month ago, and since then the number of persons arrested in connection with this affair has reached 28. When the trial was held, 16 were presented.'

Two succint comments sum up many an Islander's reaction to all these restrictions:

'We were not accustomed to being pushed and shoved about in this way'.

'We just didn't abide by what they told us and that's it.'

Rationing

FOOD

As for rationing, the increase of the population alone made it inevitable. To the 40,000 or so Jersey residents remaining were added not only the German troops – up to 11,500 on average – but also the 'slave' workers that the Germans employed to turn the Island, at Hitler's express order, into an impregnable fortress. These were foreign workers of all nationalities, directed by Dr Todt's Organisation to undertake this work of military construction, and thousands were bought into the Island at the end of 1941 onwards.

Already in October 1940 the Editor of the *Islander* had made the contrast between pre-war and the Occupation. 'Until now, Jersey has probably been one of the happiest and most prosperous communities in Europe. Now for the first time we have an unemployment problem and a feeding problem.' He went on to describe two schemes to alleviate both: peat quarried at St. Ouen and the Communal kitchen in Phillips Street. Then a whole page was given to the Relief Work at Clifton Park. 'This scheme doubtless originated in the mind of someone passing the derelict plot of land opposite the Stadium in Georgetown and conceiving the idea of growing their vegetables instead of weeds. The idea was, unlike the treatment usually accorded to bright ideas in Government Departments, taken up by the States and work commenced.'

Much more draconian measures than the Clifton Park scheme were needed, however, if the Island were to become more or less self-supporting. The States, therefore, set up an Agricultural Department which notified farmers of an immediate changeover in the use of their land. As potatoes for export were no longer needed, seed wheat from France was to take their place. This wheat was to be harvested by bringing back, with adjustments, the old type of threshing machines.

Threshed, this wheat was then taken to one of twenty storage places where it had to be raked or turned three or four times a week as there was no mechanical means of drying it. 'It took a lot of manual labour.' Once dry, it was taken to one of the States mills – 'even four of the water mills were got working, every hour that was possible'.

'Tuesday, 13th August 1940 'We go further back in time. The water mills are being mended so that we can grind our own wheat and make our own flour and because we have not much money we are going to start trading by barter. Hope we don't go back to Adam and Eve, a fig leaf apiece won't keep us very warm this winter.'

Potatoes for Island use were, of course, grown and stored in bulk in barrels. These barrels were taken to pits and stored in 10-, 15-, 20-ton divisions to allow the circulation of air. The other principal unrationed vegetables were swedes, carrots and parsnips. 'The farmers came into town on Saturday with this produce and there were always queues to get into the market.'

'The Island was sustained on wheat, potatoes and Jersey milk. Because all the flour that was ground from the wheat was pure wholemeal, that was one of the factors governing the health of the Island'.

For their part, the Germans, from the start of the Occupation imported rye flour and other goods from France for themselves. The Island's Civil Administration was also allowed to tap this continental source of supply. They formed an Essential Commodities Committee which bought and brought back to Jersey essential foodstuffs from France. But still there was not enough to go round. At the end of the second year of Occupation, in June 1942, the usual weekly ration for a Jerseyman had decreased to 3 ounces of sugar, 2 ounces of butter,

Digging waste ground in Georgetown to grow cabbages for the community. (*The Islander*, October 1940)

RELIEF WORK AT CLIFTON PARK.

Headlines portray the necessary cooperation between Occupiers and Occupied

4 ounces of meat, 5½ pints of milk, 7 ounces of of oat flour, 4½ pounds of bread and, as that was the height of the season, ten pounds of potatoes.

Monday, 2nd March 1942 'I've put on a couple of pounds in weight during the last few weeks. Now 12 stone 5 pounds, though in June 1940 I turned the scales at 16 stone.'

Tuesday, 3rd March 1942 ' – , the ex-England cricketer started work with us as a meter-reader, nothing unusual about this except that he has lost so much weight I didn't recognise him'.

'I was a teenager and went for an early morning ride to L'Etacq towing a trailer. I brought back 2 cwt of potatoes, eggs, milk, butter and home-made tobacco. When I got back into town, at the end of the journey I couldn't even raise my legs over the doorstep, I was so exhausted. One felt alright until some kind of stamina was called for.'

Eventually even milk and skimmed milk, had to be rationed. 'You used to see the whole of life in the skim milk queue, as we went up with our jugs, vases – pots of every description – to collect our ration.'

Some weeks there were much-prized extras to the usual ration. It could be a tin of green peas, rarely – a ration of red wine for adults, quite often sweets for the children. December 1942: 'Extra rations this week, ½ pint cooking oil and one tablet toilet soap'. April 1944: 'Half a pound of macaroni and half a pound of coffee substitute issued as extras'.

THE POULTRY-KEEPER'S NIGHTMARE

Cartoon from the *Evening Post*, 7th January 1941 on the theme of bartering

Sometimes the food had deteriorated before it reached the consumer, but still it was eaten. For food was the most prized essential during the Occupation.

'When I opened our semolina ration, 2 worms popped out.'

'You were lucky if your flour was clean to use. It had to be sifted for mouse droppings and shavings.'

'I had 1 pint of milk and ¼ pound butter as (birthday) presents.'

'During the Occupation I gave elocution lessons at home. One of my pupils was a farmer's boy and he asked me "Do you want money or produce?" As I had a two year old boy, I said "produce". So each week he would pay me by bringing 1 egg, 1 ounce of butter and ½ pint of milk.'

If you could afford it, there was always the black market to eke out the meagre basic ration. By the end of May 1944, not only had normal prices shot up but those 'under the counter' were exorbitant – half pound tea rose from its pre-war price of 1s. 5d. (8p) to £5, though on the black market it might be double this legitimate price. Butter, which before the war sold at 8½d. (5p) a half pound, increased to £1.3s. But 'hush hush' it could only be had for £1.10s. (80p). A sugar ration of three ounces cost 2½d; illicit sugar was as much as 16s. (80p) a pound.

'It is possible at any time to buy 'black market' meat at fancy prices and in considerable quantities if you are able to make the necessary contacts.'

'This occupation is proving to be the means of amassing large sums of money in many nefarious ways. Black market is absolutely rife; with the exception of the weekly meagre rations nothing can be got except in this illegal manner and as the period of occupation lengthens so the prices soar.'

'There is a lot of bartering going on, and black market. Though there has evidently been some of these people watching during the years of occupation, for the houses of these people have been dabbed with tar and swastikas. Just to remind them that their day is coming when they shall have to pay for their blackmarketing and co operation with the Germans.'

'Wages were not allowed to go up in the Occupation. As a married couple my husband earned £2.10s. and I earned £1.5s. With the rent of the flat to come out of that, how could we afford to buy on the black market?'

'The story is told that Coutanche the Bailiff used to go to the Animal Shelter to get meat for his dogs. Once when he was offered some meat on the black market he said, "It would be more than my life is worth".'

January 23rd 1942. 'What with the miserable weather and miserable news one feels thoroughly depressed for one is cold all the time. There are going to be only 3½ pounds of potatoes per head, per week . . . what the poor are going to do I don't know. We find things bad enough but are able to get one or two things extra at exorbitant prices, but everybody can't do this and I always feel I shouldn't do it'.

Those who did not have the means to line the purses of black marketeers, bartered. There was even an *Exchange and Mart* column in the *Evening Post* which started as early as 13th August 1940. Many are the bartering tales which those who lived through the Occupation have to tell.

This first dates from the time when the only fuel to be had was sawdust:

'It was easy to get free sawdust in the early days. Then you could only get it for 6d. (2½p) a bag. Finally it got to the stage when one after the other the saw mills closed down. All my sources of supply had dried up and I knew that there was just one place left and I went along and spoke to the foreman and said "Any chance of any sawdust?" "Sorry, we have our regular customers, we can't spare any." To which I said "Well, that's a pity because if you could have let me have some sawdust, I could have let you have some flour." "Flour?" he said, "What do you mean?" "Well, I could spare you some wholemeal flour if you could let me have some sawdust." "Well, well. Come round on Monday and we'll see what we can do," he said.'

'I had a visit by Mona to see if I could part with John's suit for her husband. I was offered money or food in exchange. I was very reluctant in parting with my husband's suit, but as I am in such desperation for bread I exchanged it for 3 pounds of wheat and some baking powder. The flour is 15s. – (75p) and £1 per pound on the black market, so the suit gets a good price. I walked to town and back the same day to complete the bargain. It is a load off my mind to have some flour to take the place of bread.'

'English money was hoarded and occasionally used for barter.'

August, 1941. 'Managed to get a pound pot of honey last week. Cost me 50 cigarettes and 2 ounces of tobacco (4s. 6d. or 22½p). Tobacco ration is now 10 cigarettes per week.'

'I needed some eggs so I said to my friend, "Let's go and see if we can barter our wellington boots for some eggs." Eventually we set off and went down to a farmer and asked if he had got any eggs. He gave us a whack of eggs and took the wellington boots. We walked back to town, then just as I was passing by the garage in Rouge Bouillon, swinging my carrier bag of eggs, I was stopped by the patrol. They took my eggs and I was put in a police cell. It was November and I was frozen in there. Luckily the Jersey policeman on duty knew me as I played football for First Tower! "Hang on a minute," he said, and gave me a police coat to wear. Next morning in the Black Maria I realised that the Reichsmarks I had on me would suggest that I was selling eggs on the black market, so I hid them under the seat. Then I was questioned as to which Parish I'd got the eggs from but I didn't want to incriminate the person who bartered with me, so I said I didn't know. Eventually they let me go, but I wanted my eggs back. "Eine moment" the German said, and handed me back my carrier bag. But there weren't as many eggs in it as before.'

'We once bartered a pair of shoes for a tree!'

'This morning Mrs Struthers managed to make a deal for me at one of the *Exchange & Mart* shops. She got me 3 pounds of sugar for ½ pound of tea. It went against the grain to part with the tea.'

'We arranged a barter with some people in the country. My husband would let them have fish during the summer and then after the harvest they would give us some wheat. We are still waiting for that wheat!'

There were even advertisements in the *Evening Post* which offered food as the reward for finding lost property. The first appeared on Saturday, 26th April 1941: 'Lost Red Horse Rug. Reward: 12 eggs. Apply *Evening Post*'.

FUEL

It was not only food, though, that was rationed. In February 1944, the fuel ration was 2 cwt coal and 1 cwt of wood per household. Next month it was the 1 cwt of wood only. In April and May there was no fuel ration at all. With cargoes of coal from France so irregular – lack of transport (not to mention Maquis sabotage and RAF bombing) was the alleged cause. Electricity and gas in Jersey were also in short supply.

In April 1944 the electricity ration was cut to 3½ units per householder per week; on May 15th the gas supply was cut down to three hours a day: 6.45–7.30 in the morning, 11.30–1.00 at lunch time and 6.15–7.00 in the evening.

'One of the exciting things in life was to find out what zone one was in when the *Evening Post* was published on a Friday, because if you were in zone A, for instance, you would be having electricity perhaps from 6.30 to 7 o'clock. That was all you would have. There was none any other time of the day. If you were in zone B, of course, it might be from 7.0 to 7.30. That was it. Half an hour's electricity a day. The rest of the time you were in darkness.'

One effort made to save fuel was the use of communal ovens – often at a nearby baker's.

'As we waited in the queue we used to ask each other "I wonder what could be in that one" as people went up to collect their baking tins.'

'One old man dropped all his roasted potatoes. So we all stopped and put them back for him.'

'We mixed the corn we made with water and salt and then took it round to the communal bake house. When it came out of the oven it was brown and hard and we had to cut it out of the tin. But if you are hungry enough you are grateful for anything. We called it "hard bake".'

'I used to cut all the vegetables up, put them in a big crock and take it to the bake house. You were given a number and it was also put on the crock. Then you would go and collect it when it was cooked.'

December 1940. 'Over two hundred people are served daily at the communal kitchen in Phillip's Street. The cost is 6d. per person and it varies from 1d. to 2d. extra for a sweet. Miss Frazer provides the best soup in the Islands.'

Tuesday, 1st April 1941. 'There was a person in the queue (at Dales in Union Street for shoes) who came with me to the Communal kitchen at St. Helier House where we obtained a meatless meal for 9d. (4½p). I enjoyed it though I could have done with another 9d. worth as we don't have the plates very full. We had tomato soup, potatoes and cabbage with a little herb cake comprising mostly of potato with herbs and after we had a little tapioca pudding which just covered the bottom of my fruit dish. This was a luxury for me as we have not been able to buy anything to make puddings with for months.'

'Soup kitchens were set up around the Island. Two such kitchens were at Valley Road and at Hillgrove Street where a bowl of hot watery vegetable soup could be obtained.'

'When I was teaching at St. Martin, the school's soup used to be brought to us by a horse and trap in used dustbins. By the time Monday's ration, which had been cooked on Friday, came to us, the children complained: "Miss, it's sour".'

The effect of the shortage of food, together with medicines, on the health of the population varied. Most people suffered from digestive troubles, wind pains known as 'Jersey Rattles' and diarrhoea. The lack of insulin meant the eventual death of the few diabetics who had not been able to take their doctor's warning to leave the Island before the Occupation began.

Friday, 17th October. 'Father has not been at all well today, in fact, not since Sunday. He is suffering from the fashionable disease every person seems to have suffered or is suffering from (diarrhoea). We had the doctor this morning and I asked him what was causing this wide-spread trouble and he said "malnutrition". I cycled 7 miles for a pint of milk last night (there and back). The doctor has given me a permit to get ½ pint of extra milk per day and ½ pound of French gruel for a fortnight.'

Saturday, 21st March 1942. 'Uncle Tom went into hospital for diabetic treatment last Wednesday. There is no more insulin for the patients, so there is only one hope, that is to undergo a diet treatment at hospital and possibly remain there till better times, when more insulin will be brought to the Islands.'

Everything had to be Wangled

'For cigarettes you used anything that dried up: rose leaf, dock, colts foot. To roll it in, perhaps toilet paper – thin Bible paper was very good. As you smoked your home-made cigarette, the first cough was heart-rendering.'

'My husband used to save all his cigarette ends so that he could remake some more. One day my son found the small tin of cigarette ends and poured the whole lot into a kettler of water that I was boiling. We lost both the precious cigarette ends and the water that had taken scarce fuel to heat. My husband was furious!'

'It was exciting to get an old dress and think what you could make out of it.'

'My mother made my father a complete suit – out of an army blanket.'

'One child in my class had a jumper knitted out of bits.'

'My two girls needed winter coats so I thought of my blackout curtains – thick, heavy and green. I got them down, washed them and took them to the dressmaker – there was twelve yards of material. She reversed the material and not only made the girls winter coats but skull caps to match. When my neighbours seemed rather envious of how smart they looked I told them they ought to come and look at our window. For the blackout they had cardboard shutters that my husband had made.'

'There used to be a secondhand shop called Yvonne's where the George Town Co-Op is now. There I saw a lady's velvet black cloak. I thought it would make my four year old son a nice rig out, so I bought it for 5 marks – 10s. 8d. (54p). His little shirt to wear under the suit was made out of a blouse of mine.'

'My son had clogs made from bicycle tyres, canvas and nails. But they were so heavy to wear that he used to go barefoot whenever possible.'

'I got a carpenter to make a handcart from my mother's table and two wheels off an old-fashioned bath chair. It had handles at the top and a place inside where a shelf could be added. I used that handcart for everything. I took the children in it to school at Grouville, walking from La Rocque and back, I used it for shopping in town and on the shelf I put the dinners that went down to the bakehouse.'

'Because I knew a girl on a farm, I used, in my time off work to help with the reaping and threshing. During the threshing the German inspectors used to be distracted so that old bags of wheat could be smuggled away. I was always given a bag of wheat to take home. Every evening we used our small coffee mill to grind it slowly bit by bit until I had an idea. I went to the grocer's and asked, "Could we use your coffee grinder?" What a difference that made!'

'Gleaning was a very tough job. I remember in that last Autumn I was gleaning in the field of a farmer friend of mine who said to me, having heard the sound of the fighting in France, "You are wasting your time, it'll be all over by Christmas". But I decided to go gleaning whatever happened and a jolly good job I did. Having gleaned this stuff, which was a very hard grain, one finished up with a great sackful of these ears of wheat which had fallen on the ground. I took them home day after day on the old bike. One would then have to push the whole great load on a hand cart up to the top of Trinity Hill which was the nearest point that a threshing machine was coming to town. I got them before they started the day's work to thresh my gleanings. It seemed terrible to me the way they were handled, with lots of little bits of corn being flung about all over the place by this machine, but that was the only way it could be done and, eventually, I finished up with a great sackful and a half of corn, which was most precious. Then, of course, it had to be ground, so every so often, having taken all that lot back home, I would take 15 or 20 kg, on the handlebars of my bike, and go up to Sion where there was a mill where a friend of mine – he had been a baker and had brought the mill back into use – would grind this wheat for me, for which I was extremely grateful.'

'Mother and I have been sitting outside on the cement thrashing our corn with sticks. It takes an awfully long time but when you're hungry you can do anything to obtain food.'

'To make sugar beet syrup, one bought a hundred weight of sugar beet and scrubbed them clean, sliced them up and cooked them in the copper in the wash-house. I was lucky that I had some friends who did some tree felling and they were able to let me have faggots of twigs, which were of no use to anybody else but very useful to me to get the copper going. Having got the beet soft, it then had to be squeezed so that all the juice came out of it – an extremely difficult job that was – and then one had to reduce all this juice by boiling it and boiling it. So after several days of hard work – and it was hard work – one finished up with about 6 or 7 jam jars full of this dark treacly stuff which one spread on a bit of hard bake, and I can assure you that that was very satisfying indeed.'

'The sugar beet had to be stirred hard to make it into syrup. So in November 1943 my husband was outside stripped to the waist stirring it. We got many jars of syrup from his efforts but he got pneumonia!'

'We had to put sea water in a saucepan and let it evaporate. We then have about two tablespoons of salt.'

'The more salt you needed the more fuel you had to use to keep boiling and boiling it – that was the problem.'

'I used to come down by bike from St. Saviour three or four times a week to go to the pool at Havre des Pas to fill two buckets with sea water. When I got home with it, as we didn't have enough fuel to boil it, we had to leave it out in the sun to evaporate. One day, catastrophe! I lost one of my buckets. The knot on the rope I used to throw it in with had undone. And the bucket had sunk where I couldn't reach it. I was severely told off!'

'My husband at a certain time of the year used to bring back howe fish, a member of the shark family. Once I had cut out the female livers, I used to simmer them gently on a wood fire and extract the oil. I had to be careful

Mr Martin Pitman with a home-made bicycle tyre from the Occupation
(*Jersey Evening Post*, December 1984)

not to cook the liver or the oil would taste fishy. The oil made lovely chips!
It was also as good as halibut oil and I gave a teaspoon each day to my
children.'

'When the potatoes weren't good enough to eat we made potato flour out
of them.'

August 1941. 'One day we borrowed a machine from Mr — of Westmount
and scraped up 140 pounds of potatoes for flour. Owing to adverse
weather it's not yet dry but I should think we have about 10 pounds of
flour. Heard of a farmer in the north who has made 1400 pounds-odd of
flour in the last few weeks.'

Friday, 18th July 1941. 'We are busy making potato flour. It is a long process but as we have nothing else to make puddings with we don't mind the bother. It makes lovely puddings just like cornflour. With 12 pounds of potatoes we made 1½ pounds flour on average.'

'Carrageen moss, an edible seaweed, was bleached on trays in the sun, then boiled and sold in packets. It was used as a blancmange, gelatine or in soup.'

Wednesday, 13th August 1941. 'Ivy and I set out to find some more seaweed or Irish Moss as some call it. We went beyond Seymour Tower before we could find any. There is great demand for it. They are making use of it also at Overdale Hospital. I understand they are also drawing some oil from it for medicine. When it is quite dry after the process of bleaching has been done, it fetches 10s. (50p) per pound so if I can get sufficient I am going to try to sell some.'

'Christmas presents for my little boy were an awful problem. But with some Carrageen moss and some chocolate from a Red Cross parcel I made him a little chocolate pudding and put it in his stocking at the foot of his bed. You should have seen the joy on his face when he discovered it – he'd never seen chocolate before!'

'People used to grow runner beans and make bean paste to put on their bread.'

'Those who lived near a slaughter house would ask for the blood and intestines of animals. With the blood they made a "black pudding" and the intestines were boiled down to a yellow fat which was then used to fry the black pudding known as "pipes and tripes".'

July 1941. 'Most of the boys at the Jersey Electricity Company including the "old man" are busy trying to perfect a method of cooking with sawdust. The chief difficulty seems to be to get the sawdust sufficiently dry. Mr — tells that he has used this method for heating and cooking for the last three years and finds it so successful that he has discarded all gas cooking and other means of heating. I'm afraid I haven't the secret yet. I cannot get my sawdust to flame for any long period. Whether this is just a question of draughts and vents or due to the fuel being wet, I'm not yet prepared to say. At the moment I am trying to find a means of enclosing the fire part so as to enable me to use a type of hot plate and so prevent the pots and pans from becoming soiled and also facilitate the refuelling and controlling of the draughts if necessary.'

'Imagine a two gallon oil drum with a hole in the bottom of it into which one inserted a piece of wood the size of a broomstick and connected it up with another piece of wood down the centre of the drum. Imagine that filled with sawdust and rammed down and then these two pieces of wood, running up through the centre of the sawdust. When these pieces of wood were removed you had this channel running through. Getting that ignited one could get a flame to come up through the hole which gradually got wider and wider, of course, as the sawdust burned away. It had a flame coming up just like a blow lamp, which gave a lovely lot of heat, and you

A paraffin lamp made from an old tin of metal polish (*Jersey Evening Post*, December 1984)

were able to boil a kettle in about ten minutes or a quarter of an hour and it gave you heat for a good many hours. If we were wanting heat for a long time we would use a 5 gallon drum which would burn all day.'

Sunday, 29th November 1942. 'Managed to get a bath today, first time for three weeks. We just cannot afford the fuel. (1 cwt coal dust and 1 cwt wood per month.)'

'To bath the kids, on a Saturday I used to get hot water from the George Town bakery – bread was steam baked in those days – and walk home with it in two buckets.'

'Having no coal, we had a shed in the yard which seemed to me would make a very good hen run. If one built up wire netting out into the yard one could put some surface there, so I went round to the gasworks and got a lot of clinker and put a layer down and built it up with wood. Then I got some soil on top of this and put up a perch inside and arranged the wire netting and went and bought a couple of hens. I bought them from a chap who assured me they were hens. We waited and waited for eggs to be laid but they turned out to be cockerels and, while they did provide some excellent meals, that was not the idea. So I went back to this chap and said "Look, those hens you sold me turned out to be cockerels." "Oh dear, I'm sorry but I've got some more here, these are hens." And so I bought these hens from him and, believe it or not, they too turned out to be cockerels! One day, a wintry day, about 4 o'clock, I came back home and my wife said, "We've just had the *Evening Post* and there are two hens for sale." Where? "St. John's". All uphill! When you've not had a lot of food and you come back tired, a cycle ride to St. John's doesn't attract, "I'd better go". To cut a long story short – we packed two very fine birds into this basket and tied them down and I set off on my bike back home. I was coming back over Mont Cochon. It was pitch dark by this time, blackout, no light anywhere and I almost ran down a German soldier, who started to shout and bawl and who, I hoped to goodness, wouldn't fire at me. So I swerved from side to side and he fortunately didn't fire. I was jolly glad when I got home. I undid this basket and out came this great white hen who obviously was highly indignant at being squashed into this basket with the other brown hen. Whitey flew up onto the table and crowed. Well, that shook us a bit! But we needn't have worried, she laid some magnificent eggs.'

Wednesday, 22nd April. 'We waste nothing! Every crumb from the table is carefully scraped up and put in a jar to make a pudding, and our potato skins are carefully washed and minced and put into potato flour. This has been going on for a long time now. We are so short rationed that we have always a craving for food.'

Growing up in Occupied Territory

One Jersey baby was nearly born in the midst of a group of German soldiers.

'My husband had called for the ambulance but when it came to the Esplanade, it turned out to be a very old one. When I was on the stretcher ready to be taken to the hospital it wouldn't start. While the ambulance men were trying to get it to go, I, still on the stretcher, was put on the pavement. Milling all round me were German soldiers on their way to the harbour to embark, complete with machine guns. Fortunately the ambulance did eventually start and I just got to the hospital in time!'

This baby's nappies, like many another's during the Occupation, were made of sheets. His father used to cycle out to a farm to get cattle liver oil to build him up. It was mixed with cow's milk, sugar beet syrup, extracted swede juice and 'looked like charcoal in the bottle!'.

The cost of children's wear during the Occupation

CHILDREN'S WEAR. "B Quality

ARTICLE		SUBSIDIZED PRICE	RETAIL PRICE	VOUCHER VALUE
	3	6d.	1/3	9d.
SOCKS	5	9d.	1/6	9d.
	7	1/–	1/9	9d.
PIXIES		1/–	1/11	11d.
JUMPERS	22″	2/1	3/6	1/5
	24″	2/6	3/11	1/5
and	26″	2/10	4/3	1/5
CARDIGANS	28″	3/1	4/6	1/5
KNICKERS	2	1/6	2/6	1/–
	3	1/11	2/11	1/–
	4	2/6	3/6	1/–
	5	2/11	3/11	1/–
PRINCESSES	22″	1/6	2/6	1/–
	24″	1/11	2/11	1/–
	26″	2/6	3/6	1/–
	28″	2/11	3/11	1/–
SLEEPING SUITS	22″	2/–	3/–	1/–
	26″	2/6	3/6	1/–
	30″	2/11	3/11	1/–
NIGHTDRESSES	30″	2/6	3/6	1/–
	34″	2/11	3/11	1/–
	38″	3/6	4/6	1/–

G. C. H. LE COCQ.
Secretary,

But as far as young children were concerned, they did not feel the deprivations of the Occupation as keenly as their teenage brothers and sisters. The ones who went without were their parents, especially their mothers. And what these youngsters had never had, they were not likely to miss.

Their pre-occupations were the same as children's have ever been: school, play and food. The only difference, was that as well as having the usual 'do's' and 'don't's' from grown-ups to put up with, they were also hedged about by enemy orders and shortages as well.

'I used to like bag-pipe music and I can still see the Philips radio on the table with me standing on a chair, gazing into the fretwork as I listened to the music. I missed it when it was taken away.'

'There were days when we couldn't go on the beach because of the sharp shooting. That was when the Germans had old cars driven on to the beach as targets. They used to shoot at them from Le Hurel Tower by La Rocque Chapel and from Le Boulevard, the biggest German gun site near us.'

'My mother spent a lot of time making me a new suit. But when she told me that she'd made it out of my aunt's skirts – I wouldn't wear it. That was women's clothes.'

As for the schools:

'During the Occupation there was a fantastic shortage of writing materials, not to mention text books. Classrooms echoed to the sound of wooden clogs made in Jersey.'

'News received by parents on hidden radios was confided by children to teachers, but never in writing. Written compositions were mostly uncommunicative.'

And towards the end when there was no heating, schools were only open two hours a day and 'you took your blanket with you'. One girl also remembers taking potatoes to school to be cooked in the school kitchen for lunch. These were recognised by having their owner's initials carved on them!

'After the evacuation there were only five children left in my class at St. Luke's.'

'I can remember when I was in the 2nd Infants at Grouville being given a soul destroying task. One teacher would cut different pieces of material from old clothes into 3 to 4 inch squares. She put these into a box and we would have to take the squares and unpick them. We all went for the loose woollen cloth ones because these were easier to unpick!'

'There would be times when I would look out of the classroom window and see the sky seemingly filled with German aeroplanes.'

Living out at St. Ouen, a boy who had started at a private school nearby and had then gone on to Victoria Prep, was delighted when

Toys made by Islanders during the Occupation

To Schoolchildren !

WANTED : ACORNS

ANY QUANTITY (large or small).

GATHER THEM IN YOUR SPARE TIME—AND RECEIVE

per **3** D. lb.

From A. C. SARRE, 30/31 Commercial Buildings, Pier

START COLLECTING NOW

Extract from the *Evening Post*, 13th October 1943

he got a scholarship to the main school. But he was not able to take up his scholarship for long because of the difficulty, at the end of the Occupation, of getting from St. Ouen to St. Saviour. So he had to go back once more to the private school close to his home.

Stanhope Landick, as a teacher himself, remembers how reluctant staff were to enforce the Order that German should be taught in school.

'The Jersey States Department of Education made desperate efforts to avoid the introduction of the German language into schools as a compulsory subject and tried many delaying tactics, including the holding of voluntary classes in German twice a week after school hours for those pupils whose parents signed a request.

The classes were not taught by Germans. The text-book chosen had been used in peace-time in schools throughout the United Kingdom, including Victoria College, Jersey. The Germans were dissatisfied with the attendance at voluntary classes and brought great pressure to bear on the Department of Education. Without informing the Germans, the Department called a mass meeting of teachers, at which all could express their views. At this very important meeting, after careful consideration of the situation, the teachers agreed very reluctantly that German would have to be a compulsory subject and that it should be taught by anyone except Germans. German became compulsory in February 1943.

The text book for German, being a copy of a British one, contained no Nazi propaganda. These books were, of necessity, poorly bound and were printed in Guernsey.

After a year of compulsory German, the States' Department of Education received from the Occupiers books to be forwarded to all schools as

Children watching German soldiers marching in the Bagot area, St Saviour

prizes for the best pupils in this subject. Every teacher of German was awarded a German book at a special ceremony on February 12 1944, attended by representatives of the Department of Education, Heads of Schools, the German Field Commandant and the German education officer. The books were left on a table for the teachers to make their choice after the ceremony. The Sonderfuhrer offered to sign the books at a later date, but very few teachers, if any, applied for this signature. One of the books was Hitler's *Mein Kampf.*'

The pupils who had to learn German decided that it was 'patriotic' not to be very good at it!

But, Occupation or no Occupation, you could still get told off. John Farley beat the transport problem by roller skating from First Tower to the Intermediate School at Brighton Road. He was late on one particular day and severely reprimanded by his teacher.

Many, looking back at their childhood between 1940 and 1945, agree that 'we made our own fun'. Often the fun had an element of danger in it, sometimes it involved avoiding or playing with the Germans.

'I used to play "Beat Your Neighbour" in the evenings with my father. As we had no electricity, we played by the light of a little bowl of lubricating oil – with a wool wick. It stank to high heaven'.

'There used to be German horses in George Town. The big ones they kept in George Town Park Estate and they were stopped running loose down Dicq Road after a request from our headmaster because of the danger to the school children. The thoroughbreds they kept in Grassette Park. They shot and skinned these just before the Liberation, because I came across their bodies when I went to play there.'

'I can remember creeping through the barbed wire along Havre des Pas to get to the beach. The soldiers were doing the same thing.'

'We used to watch the mock battles of the Germans with wooden bullets on Gorey Common. Afterwards we used to look for the empty shells to play with. Sometimes we found live ones and the older boys would put them in a vice, get a nail and a hammer and there'd be a great big bang'.

'When I was still at school, early on in the Occupation, one day we went up to the airport on our bikes with my camera that I hadn't handed in. We were lying there in the grass, keen as mustard, and we photographed some German transport planes. We had no fear – it was a bit of a dare.'

'Once there was a German guard on our front door for two and a half hours – we didn't know why. My sister didn't dare to go out past him. But I said I didn't care and I went out.'

'St. Ouen was heavily garrisoned and I used to watch the enemy manoeuvres. Our house would be the H.Q. and there was a machine gun nest outside the kitchen window.'

'I met a German soldier at my aunt's house who, when he was on guard at

Le Hurel, would let me and my cousin go in. One day I ran back home for something I'd forgotten and, when I got back to the tower, I gained entry only to be confronted by a German officer who shouted at me to get out. In my absence the friendly German had seen the officer coming and had told my cousin to run off but he didn't have a chance to warn me.'

'We knew the Germans were starving and my sister and I used to dare each other to take dead seagulls up to Le Boulevard for the Germans to eat. We used to throw them down and then run away.'

'One day we saw a German coming along with a sack. He was collecting wild spinach. My sister went to help him. When my mother asked, "Why did you do that?" she answered, "The poor man was starving".'

'There was a guilty feeling if we were too friendly with the Germans. When they wanted to join in our game of football, kicked the ball towards us, we knew it was wrong. Above my mother's bed was a picture of my father in uniform. So when the Germans tried to be friendly with us, I had to remember these were the men who were fighting my father.'

'We didn't play "English and Germans" because nobody wanted to play the Germans.'

Many young children became scavengers. 'You took it whether you needed it or not.' Girls found their knicker legs very handy but when the elastic became too loose and there was none to replace it, they used the tops of their wellington boots to hide findings.

From a window nearby a woman watched about twenty small boys down at the Weighbridge trying to steal potatoes on their way to Alderney and Guernsey. The Germans were keeping guard by going up and down the line of barrels on their bikes.

A tempting spot for St. Helier lads was Springfield, for that was where the food stores were kept. Others would go down to the pier and sweep the flour off the tops of the casks.

'We used to go in the fields and eat raw swedes.'

'One day we found a piece of a loaf of German bread lying on the ground. It had mould on it but we scraped it off and ate it – it had a sour taste.'

TEENAGERS

For teenagers, the Occupation had more serious consequences. Being cut off from England also meant being cut off from examining bodies such as the Royal Academy and the University Examining boards. So the Liberation found a whole generation who had left school without the necessary academic qualifications to start a professional career. It was five wasted years. With no Bishop in Jersey, Anglican youngsters could not even get confirmed.

Three teenagers from that time had quite different life styles and yet the all-pervasive German presence affected all three to a greater or lesser degree. The two boys came from country parishes and the girl lived in St. Helier.

One of the boys, who wanted to be a musician when he grew up, lived on a mixed farm in Trinity. He remembers the food from the farm being taken by horse transport into a central depot in town and it being distributed from there to both Germans and Jerseymen.

'Once out in Trinity I saw a British plane fly over, being fired at by the Germans. There was shrapnel everywhere, so I ran into a farm yard to take shelter. When I got there it was full of Germans.'

While school buses ran he used them, after that he went by bike. Although he did not have to learn German, he does remember Germans coming to inspect his school. But for him his school days are marked by there being no academic or music exams.

'For me that was a tremendous handicap. People of that period had to start their careers later.

In fact the year after the Liberation the Associated Music Board gave youngsters like me a chance to catch up. They held their exams in the January and the March of that year. So I took four music exams in the space of three months.'

But how did his music teacher manage for pieces to practise?

'Mostly the teachers found us something to play, but my own teacher, as well as being paid for the lessons in Reichsmarks, also requested a couple of logs to keep the fire going.

I also learnt the cello and my first experience of playing in an orchestra was in Handel's *Messiah* put on at the Methodist Chapel in the Royal Crescent by Mr P. G. Larbalestier. There were some Germans among the audience and when the audience all rose in silence, as is the custom for the Halleluiah Chorus, one German in uniform stood up and sang the whole chorus through in German. The rest of the audience looked round, wondering where the voice was coming from.

Then there was the time when I was going to play the piano at a concert put on in St. Clement's Parish Hall. As usual the programme had to be submitted to the German censor. I had chosen one of Mendelssohn's *Songs without Words* but because Mendelssohn was a Jew the piece couldn't be played. The Germans used to go very strictly into some details like that. So I had to play Schubert's *Impromptu* – a bother to me because it was more difficult!'

In 1942 Percy Hembest joined the St. John Ambulance Brigade – the only uniformed organisation that the Germans allowed.

'When some German ships went down and the bodies of the crew were washed ashore, the coffins of the Protestants were laid to rest in St. Luke's Church. I formed part of the Guard of Honour that kept a two hour vigil beside the coffins before they were buried.'

As well as taking part in the normal Parade Nights, training and

Occupation entertainment

competitions, this young man also stood in as part time nursing auxiliary at the General Hospital. 'The first time I was there, I assisted a nurse to insert a catheter into a man with gonorrhea.'

At weekends he used to walk into town from St. Ouen to go to the Cinema. 'There were a few old English films still left but I also remember seeing a film at the Forum which starred Marika Röek – Hitler's favourite actress.' The music he associates with that period of his life is also German. 'I shall never forget the tunes the Germans sang as they marched down the roads – three tunes in particular.'

For a girl who was brought up in St. Helier during the Occupation, a visit to the country was something of an excitement:

'Sometimes we cycled to a farm at Mont Mado and stayed there overnight. Mum cooked rock buns for us to take and we brought back farm stuff on our bikes. When we slept there, we lay on the floor all in a row.'

Another attraction of the country for her were horses:

'A friend of Dad's had a farm and a few horses. I pestered to go for so long,

Occupation entertainment

that at last my father asked the farmer, "Give my daughter something to do". I was given the job of mucking out. So I would cycle to Maufant, muck out the horses and be given a ride. But one day the Germans had put some of their horses in the stables and I saw a very good looking German officer exercising his horse. I saw him twice, though, of course, I never spoke to him. Then all the visits to the farm stopped. I don't think my father liked the idea of Germans being at the stable while I was there.

We used to have a wireless. Then Dad got a bit worried. "We've got to get rid of this", he said. A few weeks later there was a banging at the door. Dad got up and we were on the staircase as he opened the front door. "Come, come" said the German, and led him across the road. "Where are you taking him?" my mother called out. When my father got to the other side of the road, the German pointed up to the attic of our house. My brother's room was showing a glimmer of light!'

In town her amusement was dancing:

'I belonged to the Fifty-Fifty Club. I was in the dancing corps with my sister – I got roped in. Then there were dancing lessons at Swanson's Hotel. That was when I nearly got caught after Curfew. My brother wanted to come with two friends and afterwards we all stopped chatting. Suddenly we realised we only had two minutes to get home. "You've got to take your shoes off", said my brother, "and run, but if you're seen, just walk casually". Then we spotted a German guard coming our way, so we had to hide in an alley in New Street. Luckily he went straight into Burrard Street. When he'd gone, we ran home barefoot. I was more worried about what my father would say about me getting home late, than meeting a German!

My eldest brother met the Curfew problem by always having his watch a few minutes slow. One night, after he should have been indoors, he was walking home when he saw some German soldiers looking his way. He carried on walking slowly and whistling. When they approched him, he pointed at his watch. But this time it didn't work. They walked him home. "I've been caught at last", he said, as he got in.

The last year of the Occupation got boring. You knew all your own clique. You were tired of the local boys. The German officers looked very attractive and they made me keep thinking of their British equivalents.'

Tales from Town

'People in the country were better off than the townspeople.'

'It was difficult for people who were working and lived in flats. They had nowhere to grow vegetables and they had no time or energy to go gleaning.'

These two comments are typical of townees, who thought that those living in the country parishes were far less affected by the Occupation than those living and working in St. Helier. So what was it like to live and work in town?

Miss Izette Croad kept house for her father and brother in Colomberie and attended St. Columba's Church in Midvale Road, whose minister was the Revd. Struthers. She also kept a diary throughout the Occupation. These extracts, leading up to the first Christmas under German rule, provide an interesting comparison with Mrs Bullen's description of how her family spent the last Christmas before Liberation Day, which is found in the next chapter:

Tuesday, 10th December. 'Notice in *Evening Post* that there is to be a Concert of Advent Music given by the German Marines at the Town Church tomorrow evening, to which the civil population are cordially invited. We are bombed at Midsummer and serenaded at Christmas! I shall not go tho' I should love to hear the music, but could not be happy there while bombs will no doubt be falling on the U.K.'

Thursday, 19th December. 'Special ration from Le Riche today for registered customers; ½ pound of ground almonds and ½ pound of nuts. We have acquired 2 pounds of extra butter and 3 Camemberts this week. I had some of the butter and cheese and Mrs Struthers some butter, the rest I am keeping for Christmas to make a few rock cakes. The Swastika was flying from the Fort yesterday, the weather was dry. When it rains no flags are flown, the black Swastika apparently runs into the white circle and so does the red. It would take more than Jersey rain to make the colours of the Union Jack run!'

Christmas Eve. 'At Le Riche this afternoon there was nothing for sale except some tins of grapefruit and packets of tea (the latter only with coupons), and a few tins of Jersey produce, peas, tomatoes, etc. Father got a piece of Cheddar and also about ½ pound of mixed chocolates, but neither of these were on view and were evidently kept for the oldest customer, we being perhaps the oldest, even unto the 5th generation! I have managed to get 2 fowls, one, about the size of a sparrow, is to be eaten tomorrow and the other on Sunday. One which cost 9s. (45p) I took to the butcher to be cleaned and trussed and he promptly offered me £1.10 for it, and today he wanted to buy half my piece of pork which I had acquired. There was a board outside a shop in the French Lane this afternoon stating they were willing to exchange a goose for 50 cigars and a rabbit for a box of chocolates. Curfew is extended till 3 a.m. Have had another ½ pound butter so have roasted potatoes in their jackets under the dining room fire and have eaten them with, I am ashamed to say how much butter. Mrs Struthers 'phoned this evening to ask if we would like a Camembert. She will bring it to Church on Sunday morning so it is to be hoped it is a mild one.'

Christmas Day. 'And everybody gets greetings except the Channel islanders. The King of Norway sends greetings to his people, as does the Queen of Holland to hers, but the only British people in occupied territory get none. Not a word over the air to give us a little cheer on this Christmas Day of 1940. Aunt came to dinner, fowl tho' small was very good. The rest of the family came at 6 o'clock for supper – tinned soup, tongue out of a glass, bought months ago, and salad, Christmas pudding, cheese and biscuits (hoarded since July) and coffee. Have been on my feet all day.'

WORKERS IN TOWN

Then there are tales from some of those who worked in town. These range from manning an essential service, through serving behind the scenes, or the counter, of a bank, post office and grocer's, to knitting in a factory.

Mr Burrell, who was the Engineer and Manager of the Jersey Electricity Company, explains the position of the essential services in the *Electrical Review*, June 1945:

'The States placed the control of their Telephone Department, also the gas, waterworks and electricity companies, in the hands of the Department of Essential Services. This Department was composed of three members of the States, with the gas and waterworks company's engineers and myself acting as technical advisers, an arrangement which worked very smoothly, as we all had one object in view and one object only, namely to act as a buffer between the Germans and the civil population.

They brought an electricity rationing scheme with them which allowed each household three lights and one fire, but all other apparatus was to be removed. However, we managed to squash this, and got them to agree to each consumer's electricity consumption being reduced to 66 per cent of his pre-war figure. This scheme remained in force until March 1943, but many of our consumers had exceeded their rations, and the Germans were beginning to examine the meter cards, so we changed the scheme and carried out the domestic rationing on a household group basis, thereby giving our people a clean sheet. The new basic ration for lighting and ironing was 3½ units per household per week during the summer months, and 5 units a week for the winter months, but the Department of Essential Services was allowed to grant licences for the use of domestic appliances, and the additional current involved, on receipt of doctors' certificates, and this enabled us to avoid a great deal of hardship where consumers had illness in the house. Except in cases of very severe illness,

69

Occupation currency

all these licences were cancelled at the beginning of September 1944, when electric cooking was also ordered to cease, at the same time as the gas supply terminated.

During the last twelve months the Germans reduced the domestic ration in stages, until in January 1945, they finally brought it down to one unit per household per week, quite oblivious of the fact that the supply would cease long before we had any check on consumers. Incidentally, during the last five months we had a constant series of conflicting orders, and arguments with the Germans as to how the remaining fuel supplies should be dealt with.'

One effect of the cutting of communications with the mainland was immediate. As Mr J. Thuiller – who had worked first in the Library Place branch of Lloyds in Jersey before being transferred to Guernsey – noted in a recent speech to the Channel Islands

Occupation Society reported in the Jersey *Evening Post*, 'The banks had to attain an almost independent status.'

He went on to explain the expertise in exchange rates needed by all bank staff in those days:

'At this time the remaining English money in the Islands was supplemented by large quantities of marks being brought in by the German forces. This was in addition to francs, and all bank employees had to be conversant with the exchange rate. The general lack of sterling prompted both Jersey and Guernsey to introduce their own coins at this time.

Always fearing for the security of items remaining in the Islands in the banks' strongrooms and suspecting that the Germans might raid all safety deposit boxes, it befell more senior staff to attempt to secrete items they knew to be of value away from their particular bank. This included not only small items of jewellery, money and the like, left by customers, but all the mess plate of the Royal Irish Fusiliers (the Regiment had left Jersey shortly before the Occupation). An urgent communication to the Island immediately after Liberation was to make sure that their cherished mess plate was safe. Thanks to the diligence of the bank staff, it was, having been hidden for the duration in a manager's house.'

A former counter clerk at the main Post Office in Broad Street remembers that the States had to take over the payment of Old Age and Army Pensions, formerly dealt with from England. He also remembers to this day the colours of the paper Reichsmarks he had to handle: the green ½ Reichsmark, the brown 1 Reichsmark, and the blue 5 Reichsmark.

Then to his usual duties were added two others, not so usual:

'First I had to learn to count in German. Later on, when our large stock of English 1d. stamps ran out, we had to cut the 2d. stamps in half, diagonally, and use those. Before the end of the Occupation, however, Jersey began printing its own stamps – next door to us, at Bigwoods.'

The look and feel of all the shops in town was bleak, as this comment describes.

20th January 1942. 'Went to de Gruchy to pay a bill and it was like walking into a refrigerator. There is no heating of course but wonder why it feels colder inside.'

Two welcoming and welcomed focal points in town, though, were the Red Cross Post Office in Beresford Street and the *Evening Post* on the corner of Charles Street and Bath Street.

'It certainly is a thrill to receive a Red Cross letter. We know because we have received one. Congratulations to all the people responsible for this wonderful service.'

'In our Red Cross letters we used to say, "The greenfly are not too bad this year" when we wanted to tell our families and friends in England that so far we had not had any trouble from the Germans.'

And if anyone knew what was going to happen before it did, it was the staff at the *Evening Post*. They were always ready with an advance warning to neighbours of what the next Order would clamp down on or commandeer.

Many are the tales that could be told by Mr R. G. Riches, who during the five years of the Occupation was Manager of the R. M. Stores, the largest ration retailers in Jersey. The following extracts come from an article he wrote and from a subsequent interview for the *Islander* Magazine:

'On the morning after the Occupation I was at my business early as the Bailiff had made an appeal the previous evening asking everybody to carry on and keep cool and dignified.

During the morning two slimy, heel-clicking Nazis came into the shop and I received them in my office. They asked me what stocks we had and said they wished to look over the premises.

After they had done so they peremptorily announced that they were

A German officer oversees the printing of the *Evening Post*

going to requisition half of our goods, and later came with labels bearing these words in German, "Reserved for Luftwaffe"

Directly they had gone I gave orders to my assistants who lost no time in removing as much of our stocks as they could to different farms in the country. This caused a good deal of anxiety as we naturally didn't know which farms might be requisitioned. My one concern was to ensure that Nazi "half-share" should be as small as possible by the time they came to take stock!

They didn't come until the afternoon by which time a considerable amount of our stock had been removed.

Each month we had to make a return of stocks for the Germans, but the stuff we had "planted" enabled us to help our customers for quite a time.

We gradually got used to having to serve Huns (locally they were known as "Greenflies" or "Locusts") but it was galling, nevertheless, to see them purchasing some of our best lines.

Quite a common occurrence was for an officer to produce a permit entitling him to a 100 pound chest of tea. Insult was added to injury by them driving away in a car which belonged to me, but had, like more of

Burton's – requisitioned by the Germans to sell inexpensive goods to their troops

our possessions, been requisitioned.

There were many instances of the customers NOT always being right in the eyes of our assistants and innumerable complaints and threats were received. One such complaint was caused by the following amusing incident. It will be recalled that Fry's used to give away coupons in their tins of cocoa, and so many coupons entitled a person to a box of chocolates. The first Nazi to come and ask for his box was told by me to keep the coupons and apply for it directly he reached London! This incident was reported.

Although we were receiving a few goods from France, most of our tinned stuff was disappearing.

Sometimes I got hold of a French Skipper and gave him money, but it was all a question of trust and luck. In this way, however, we got butter, flour, sugar, Camembert cheese, macaroni and tunny fish.

All the time things were getting tighter. Before the war we had 28 vans, and of the five left us by the Nazis only two were allowed on the road. No longer was a house to house service possible. Goods were taken to Depots in the country by bicycles which had tyres made from garden hose pipe!

Then bags and paper supplies ran out, although a local firm did its best to.cope with this situation. Toilet rolls were made from paper used in the packing of tomatoes.

The money problem was a very real one since we had to reckon in Reichsmarks (2s. 1½d.) and francs (20 to 1 Reichsmark). Although all English money had been withdrawn, Jersey notes were issued for 6d., 1s., 2s., 10s. and £1.

It is hard for us to believe that at one time we had only three items for sale. These were a ration of 5 pounds of potatoes, 6 ounces breakfast meal (mainly husks) and sugar for bottle fed babies only. Occasionally we had sugar beet syrup which sold at 5s. 6d. (27½p) per pound.

There was no gas, no electricity, no candles. No laundries, no soap, no hot water, no brushes. Necessity being the mother of invention we set to and made such things as rope brushes, and at one period we were selling tomato box kindling over our bacon counter. Clothes pegs were made from wire – salt was home produced. On one occasion there was a glut of whitebait and we used every conceivable contrivance to secure a big catch. These were sold – and did they prove acceptable to our customers!

When war broke out we had a staff of forty-three, but after the evacuation only three remained. Further staff had been secured, when we were again depleted by the deportation.

Our travellers kept calling on country customers – hard work indeed on solid tyres!

By a Nazi order prices were not to be raised, and our hours were from 10 to 12 and 2 to 4.

At the worst period robberies were prevalent, and we used to securely bolt and bar all doors from inside and then let ourselves into the street by descending from a ladder dropped from a first floor window.'

Mr Riches particularly relishes the memory of two notices he put in his shop window. The first read 'Jersey Bags Strong and Reliable –

Occupation restrictions

A German soldier and Jersey policemen at the weighbridge, St Helier

1 mark', whose meaning had an extra dimension when one remembers that girls who fraternised with the enemy were known as 'Jerry bags'. Then, shortly after the news that the German boat *Scharnhorst* had been sunk, he claimed for a French bouillon cube he had for sale that it 'Stops that Sinking Feeling'.

Miss Hilda Marrett had the misfortune to lose her job at Woolworth's, when it closed down – nothing more to sell – after the first six months of the Occupation.

'The remnants of Woolworth's stock were sold in the shop opposite and the three youngest girls and one clerk were kept on there. The rest of the staff were dismissed. The Germans then walked into Woolworth's, took over the building and used it as a military stores.

I was afraid to ask for a job in case I got sent to a German house, so I went to see the Vicar of St. James, the Revd. Flloyd. After I had told him that we'd all been sacked he said, 'I shall see the Bailiff about this'. Shortly afterwards a notice was given out forbidding any managers to close their businesses or to sack their staff. Everybody who had already been displaced had to go to Church House.

When I got there, there was a long queue and they took my name and address. Within two weeks I was asked to see two ladies from Summerland. One was from the factory itself and the other was from the States. "Can you knit?" I was asked. "Yes". "There will be no written instructions for what you knit, you'll have to remember".

So I was given number 11 steel needles and some 4-ply wool, told how many stitches to cast on, how many inches of rib to knit and how to turn the heel by a special method. So I started knitting my first pair of socks. Every morning five more ladies were added until we were 25 by the end of the week. Then our work was examined by a French lady and she said, "The best is Miss Marrett".

Then we were divided into four classes, all making socks and I taught knitting to a class of 25. We made gentlemen's socks by hand, grey mostly, and our hours were from 9 to 6.

I had been working there about six months when this female clerk from Woolworth's sent for as many former staff as she could find to meet at her house. The German Commandant had been to see the boss and had said, "Now we have no big store to go to with 3d. or 6d. articles, I command you to open another. We can get you stocks through France. Ask your former staff to come and run the business." The clerk pointed out that we'd get more wages than we got at Summerland. But I said, "No, I'm very sorry, I won't go." Though my brother warned me to be careful what I said, I wrote a letter to my former boss explaining. "The States has trained me for a special job and I must stay in it." The Germans then took over Burton's Store – it was only for the Germans – and they white-washed the windows. They were served by ex-Woolworth's girls.

I was only paid enough to buy my rations. I couldn't afford to buy the stockings we were allocated.'

Many people had cause to be thankful for the co-operation between the workers of Summerland and the States during the Occupation. The unemployed found jobs and the consumers had a supply of clothes and clogs to buy.

Tuesday, 26th May 1942. 'We are thankful that a little of the most necessary clothes are made at Summerland Factory which the States have taken over. Most of the garments are made from clothes of evacuated houses.'

One man's job in town meant that part of the time he had to work with a German:

'The Department of Labour made me an inspector to decide which trees should be cut down for fuel. At that time no-one could cut down a tree, even if it was your own tree, not even the Germans, without a permit. I was supplied with a bike, met my German opposite number at the Department and we would cycle off to wherever the next trees would be felled. He put a swastika on trees the Germans wanted and I put a number on ours. They always used the best trees.

Then, when somebody who wanted wood applied to the Department of Labour, they were told which field and which number tree to go to. The whole family would arrive for the felling with prams and bikes to cart the wood back to town. Even the sawdust was picked up and put into bags.

The German Inspector had a job and I had a job to do and we did it. It was the only way the public could legitimately get fuel. I got paid £2.10s. a week as a married man; 15s. went for the rent and 2s. would buy rations for two.'

Some people, however, refused absolutely to work with or for the Germans:

'My father had a saw mill. One day he was asked by the Germans to saw up some tyres to repair the soldiers' boots. He refused. They took over the saw mill.'

'The Germans paid for the use of the lorry but no one was willing to drive it for them, so the Germans had to provide their own driver. When the Commandant wanted to know why a Jersey driver couldn't be found, the owner of the lorry sent his manager to explain. He couldn't trust himself to hold his tongue. The manager told the Commandant "We've only got one driver and he's sick".'

Two nice observations made about St. Helier highlight the scarcity of luxuries as well as the scavenging propensities of the townees. As early as December 1940 it was noticed, 'The streets are looking much cleaner and tidier owing to the absence of chocolate wrapper covers and cigarette boxes littering up the gutters, roadways and pavements.'

'One day in November there was a terrible storm. Westmount was like a heaving mound of ants. Everyone was searching the ground for fallen branches, cones, anything that would burn.'

But even the Occupation could not stifle the townee's sense of humour:

Thursday, 26th March 1942. 'When I went to de Guerins Library this morning I saw a notice up in big black letters. "If any reader in this Library finds any passage in any book of anti-German character please inform the Librarian, Thank you." Can you imagine any normal person rushing round pointing out passages in different books. It is a good thing there is something to make one smile occasionally.'

Out of Town

'The goodwill of the farmers was excellent. They adapted themselves remarkably well.'

The main adaptation was from being exporters of potatoes and tomatoes to becoming growers of wheat and vegetables. But the pride of Jersey's agricultural industry was then, as it had been from as far back as the eighteenth century, its dairy herd – the gentle Jerseys with their doe-like eyes, 'supreme for the production of milk, butterfat and protein'.

Included in the Orders governing the Island during the Occupation however, were 'laws requisitioning hundreds of animals for slaughter'. So, 'along with the strict control of the registration of calves, the Island herd dropped dramatically in numbers'. Fortunately for the future strength of the breed, the selection for that slaughter was allowed to remain in the hands of the Royal Jersey Agricultural and Horticultural Society and so 'mainly inferior animals were taken'.

However, it was a close thing, as the RJA & HS Centenary report points out. 'Towards the end of the War, the number of cattle selected for slaughter was increased and had the war continued for many more months there may not have been any cattle left on the Island. In reality, the slaughter of inferior stock left the Island with a nucleus of prime breeding stock, and at the first show following the War, the Island had one of the best shows in its history.'

Interestingly enough, the Germans too wanted to stage a cattle show in Jersey – for propaganda purposes. But because of all the insuperable difficulties suggested by the farming community in putting on such a show, it never materialised.

A potential threat to the purity of the Jersey breed came from the importation, prohibited both before and after the war, of an alien breed. But fortunately, no inter-breeding took place.

June 1942: 'Quite a number of foreign cattle have been brought over for consumption by Germans and civilians and they are herded in fields in different parts of the island. What ugly brutes they are compared to our own breed of cows. They don't taste so good either, even old boots would be tastier and more tender than our present day meat ration (still 4 ounces).'

The cattle food for all herds – in those days the biggest herd of Jerseys would have been about twenty-four – came from France and was given by the Corn Trade Association to the Corn merchants for distribution in proportion to the number of head of cattle. The farmers would collect their allocation of linseed cake, or ground nut cake if available, from the Parish Halls. Sometimes there would be nothing for two weeks, but when the cattle food did come, the atmosphere in the Parish Halls, with all the local farmers there, was 'like a fair'.

One animal that had an instant and incredible increase in popularity was the pig. V. J. Bailhache sums up the porcine position in these words, 'When people of Jersey look back upon the Occupation period, they will associate it with PIGS!' He goes on to say:

'The farmers complained that the price offered for the animal did not pay for its raising and consequently the number of pigs kept for slaughter decreased considerably. There were those, however, who would eat roast pork regardless of price, and consequently the black market in pigs was a lucrative trade. Only the unregistered pigs could find their way into the black market – one must except the stolen pigs which always ended their career in the same way – with the result that scores of pigs in Jersey found a lodging with people, who, prior to the war did not know the tail from the snout of such an animal.'

One stolen pig gave an unexpected feast to Mrs Bullen and her neighbours in the La Rocque area:

Mr Baudains, the local vet, in his horse and cart

'During the night of the 8 December (1943) Mr Gibaut lost a sow. The thieves had stunned it in the sty and tried to drag it away but the dog must have disturbed them, for it was found dead a few yards away in the morning. So by the time the police and veterinary surgeon were informed, precious time in which the pig should have been bled was wasted and therefore the pig bled very little. The pork was not in A1 condition, therefore they had the order to sell it amongst the neighbours as it wouldn't keep, so there was great excitement as we all went for our slice. We had about two pounds and as there was no meat ration this week (as is often the case) it came in very useful. We had not had such a dinner for nearly four years.'

There is also a delightful tale told, springing from the fact that all dead animals had to be verified by a vet, of one vet having a spate of calls to certify the death of a sow in different parts of the Island. Each certificate he gave covered the consequent pork feast should any questions be asked. But the vet became suspicious that he was being asked to certify the same animal, being passed from one farmer to another. So he marked the sow and the spate of calls ended as suddenly as they had begun.

One man who grew up on a farm in Trinity remembers the regular inspections carried out by the Germans:

'They used to come round looking for wheat. We had some of our surplus buried under the floor, some hidden in cider casks. At the top of the casks were the apples, at the bottom the wheat. We were very nervous at the time of the inspections but nothing was ever found. One of those who came to inspect was a Dutchman. As he was almost as much on our side, he was not very particular in his searching and he used to hand round cigarettes. We were just lucky.'

Another time the Germans turned up one morning in the yard of the Trinity farm for a different reason:

'They wanted somewhere for their horses. They put them into our stables. We daren't say anything. No permission was asked. One chap with a machine gun was in the front garden – standing on top of the spot where I'd buried my camera!'

But there was camaraderie in that part of the country – Augres Post Office was a telephone exchange that could be trusted. Many were the phone calls between the twenty five subscribers in that area if they were unable to visit each other.

Claude Horman's father was a merchant on the Esplanade but when the business was taken over by the Germans and run by only a skeleton staff, his two sons had to look elsewhere for employment. They went to work a mixed farm at Mont Mado, in the parish of St. John. Immediately they were in business, the Germans began their regular inspections:

'They came in the early morning to test the cows to see how much milk they were yielding and to weigh the milk. But I got up at 1 o'clock each morning to milk the cows before the Germans came. I hid the milk to use as a form of bartering.'

Pigs were part of Claude Horman's farming programme too:

'If you raised pigs, they had to be registered and go down to the abattoir to be slaughtered. So of the ten pigs we had, we registered eight and kept two for ourselves. One day our two little beggars shot off. I heard someone shout "Claude, your two pigs are going down Bonne Nuit Hill". Now the Germans had a garrison there, so I chased after the pigs. I just managed to stop them. It was a close shave! As the pigs were unregistered, I couldn't have complained that they were gone!'

Another time Claude Horman's quarry was not pigs but rabbits:

'I saw that the Germans had some rabbits in hutches and so I decided for the sake of the adventure – I didn't want to be stuck in Jersey away from the fighting – that I would take some. I took a sack and got hold of ten rabbits. When I came back to my girlfriend's, farm I let them all out in the kitchen. When she saw what I'd done she was terrified and told me to get rid of them or I'd be in trouble. So I put them all back in the sack and bartered them. In exchange I got a bag of wheat. As I was walking away with my wheat, I was stopped by a German "Halt". But I shot off with the German following me on a small bike. The first turning I went down I chucked the wheat over the hedge. At five o'clock that same day I went to get the wheat back and hid it in the attic. But the day after the Germans came, found the wheat, took it away – but they gave me a receipt.'

Having plenty of land to grow crops did not mean, as farmer Joseph Boleat' discovered, that during the Occupation it was used necessarily for that purpose. Around his farm house in St. Saviour were gradually dug 52 manholes, 5 underground bunkers, 1 ammunition dump and one gun shelter. No wonder that his son remembers that as well as three German horses in their stables, 'we had a guard on duty round the farm day and night'.

Yet, incredibly, the family managed to keep one lorry and one T Ford out of German hands all that time. A little tinkering with the lorry's engine by a kind neighbour and when the German's came to commandeer the lorry it would not budge. 'Then we put it in our shed, took off the wheels and sides, and loaded it with bales of straw so that it was covered and wouldn't be noticed.'

'The T Ford was parked in the top shed of the farm. You only had to lift the latch of the third door along and there it was. But the German who came looking to see what we'd got that we shouldn't have, walked into the press house at the front end of the shed and didn't think of going any further. The T Ford remained where it was and was never discovered. But the day before Liberation, I remember my Dad asked the German horse-driver, who'd lived in a wooden house at the back of the farm, to come and have a look at what had been hidden from them all that time. You had to be smart in those days!'

'The Germans on our farm were very nice, they were no trouble at all. We allowed them to cook potatoes behind their officer's back. In return they put a ½ ton of coal in the pigsty and told my sisters to take a couple of shovels full of coal only now and then so that attention would not be drawn to it.'

But there was a limit as to how much the Boleats could complain about the soldiers' behaviour:

'My father made a chicken-run. It disappeared one night and later he saw it in Green Farm, which was used by the Germans for guns which they would fire across to Normandy. He didn't think it worth his while to try to get it back. Also the Germans on our farm used to milk the cows of our neighbour in the middle of the night and hide the milk in our loft – there was nothing we could do about it.'

There was often fun as well down on the farms:

'We used to have cider parties at each other's farms and I used to do a Russian dance to the tune of *Roll out the barrel* played on the accordion.'

Farmers were not the only ones to earn their living out of town, there were the fishermen too. They were even more hedged about with restrictions. Harbour Control was taken over by the Germans as early as 16th July 1940, and all fishermen had to get their permits from them.

April 1941. 'The fishermen have had new orders. They have to pay the Germans a deposit on their boats. £10 on motor or sailing boats and £5 on little yawls, and they can only go from Gorey, St. Helier or St. Aubin's Harbours for their fishing. In addition to this, all boats whatever size, whether they are stored in garages etc. must be taken to these harbours under a severe penalty. It is obvious that they are still afraid that some boats might escape and so they are cunning and use tactics which makes us like children under their commands.'

A month later permission was given to fishermen to fish from La Rocque Harbour, instead of having to go all the way round the coast to Gorey, on the payment of a £2 deposit.

'They have very strict regulations to keep and always a special guard on them but with all this we see no fish whatsoever as the Germans try to get the fish as the boats arrive. The catches are very small as they can only go two miles out.'

In the September of that year Miss Croad's brother was allowed to go even further – to a part of Grouville Parish, fifteen miles south of Jersey:

'E. has been to Les Minquiers. They had to take two Germans with them

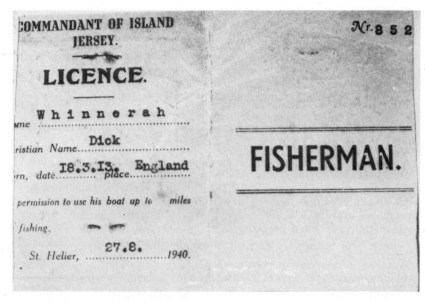

COMMANDANT OF ISLAND
JERSEY.

Nr. 8 5 2

LICENCE.

Name ...... W h i n n e r a h ......

Christian Name...... Dick ......

Born, date...... 18.3.13. place...... England ......

FISHERMAN.

permission to use his boat up to ... miles

fishing.

St. Helier, ... 27.8. ......1940.

1940 fisherman's licence

as guards, each armed with loaded revolvers of course. They were two boys aged 17 and 19. One spoke English very well. There were a lot of mackerel about and one of them amused himself by trying to shoot some. What was most annoying was the amount of food they had, including simply loads of butter, Camembert cheese (which we had not seen for about two months) and, of course, German sausage. E. had taken ½-dozen apples and they had no fruit and they were not offered any.'

Then in June 1942 came strict instructions as to how boats were to be painted:

27th June 1942. 'German Order issued whereby all fishing boats must, before 5 July, be painted with the colours blue, white and red, in that order, from the bows, across the boats' sides and foredecks, extending from the waterline on one side to the waterline on the other, each strip to be a foot wide.'

Mrs de Gruchy's husband was a fisherman and she has a tale to tell of those days:

'My husband had to have a special permit to fish from St. Helier harbour. One soldier always went with them on the fishing trips and when they got back their catch was inspected by a German and a civilian inspector. Twenty per cent of the fish went to the Germans, ten per cent he was allowed to bring back to his family and the rest to the market.

84

Once my husband and a friend were informed on because they hadn't declared their catch. They had to go up to College House to answer the charge. They were represented by a solicitor and they got off – the informer had given the wrong date. Not only did they not have to pay the fine but their solicitor wouldn't charge them either.'

The Germans, though, were not only watching the coasts for escapees, they also had other suspicions of those who lived by the sea as Mrs Bullen, who lived at La Rocque, noted in her diary:

Tuesday, 15th October 1940. 'I went to town the afternoon and heard a most distressing rumour that we were to be shifted from our house on the sealine because the Germans had an idea that some people are signalling to British planes at night but so far have heard no orders about it.'

Thankfully nothing came of that rumour. Nearly a year later though, some householders on the coast of Grouville were not so fortunate:

Tuesday, 5th August. 'Went for a picnic to Gorey Village and took the bus as far as Grouville as it goes no further. As we were walking the rest of the way we could see men busy pulling down the bungalows on Grouville Common which is by German orders that they have to be down within a limited time. On Tuesday we had a shock with the news that the Misses S.— had had a notice that they had to quit their own home in five days as it was to be demolished. Such news gives those concerned a shock especially when it is their property. Mrs B. of Le Boulevard has also had a similar notice. The Misses S.— have, through their lawyers, pleaded for twelve days and had it granted for themselves and Mrs B. through the Commandant. They have taken over Broomfield near La Rocque Post Office and Mother has had a busy week getting the house ready.'

The German coastal watch in St Ouen, looking towards Corbiere

Sunday, 20th June to Saturday, 26th June: 'Nothing unusual. A busy week at Rockleaze. The moving has to be done by horse and van and the vans are small which takes much longer.'

The vital link between coast and country and town was transport. Once the Germans had commandeered most cars and lorries, therefore, both the general public and commerce had to look to other methods of getting about. The public depended on the buses. There was even at one point a Town Bus Service with fares at 2d. and 3d. But all bus services gradually dwindled. For instance in 1941, the Grouville area was served by four buses a day, the last one leaving town at 5.00 p.m. By 1944 the buses only ran once a day – 10.00 a.m. from Grouville, returning from town at 5.15 p.m. – and those ran on charcoal. Before the end of the Occupation all buses stopped. Then the alternatives, whatever the distance, were cycle or shank's pony.

The lorries that commerce depended on were also eventually converted to gasogene. For the conversion a seven foot cylinder fuelled and fired by charcoal was fitted to a wing of each vehicle. When there was no more charcoal, locally-made wooden blocks were used. The engines had to be converted too.

To make the fullest use of each fuel-consuming journey, ten–twelve ton horse trailers were often fitted to the lorries. These were formerly horse drawn trolleys modified – but without the shafts. These makeshift trailers did their job but by the time they had transported goods from St. Helier to the top of St. Aubin's Hill, their wheels had heated up to such an extent that they had to be cooled down. Fashioned in the age of the horse, they were not made to go fast. The remedy was to take jerry cans of water on the lorry to cool down the hubs whenever necessary.

When no lorry was available even handcarts were used for the carrying of essential goods. When two men were sent off from St. Helier to Gorey with a handcart of produce, 'one of them had blisters so big on his feet that he could no longer walk. So he came back in the handcart!'.

What life was like out of town in the last few months of the Occupation can be seen from the following extracts. They come from a diary Mrs Iris Bullen kept from 1940–1945 while she brought up her children in her mother's house on La Rocque coast road when her husband was in the British army. As early as October, 1940 she was writing, 'Oh for the day when we can get those things we miss so much! We are just keeping body and soul together now.' How much worse were the privations she was writing about four years later:

17th September to 8th October 1944. 'We are struggling along in our everyday life and making the best of it. Have heard that the Commandant of the Islands was approached by the Allies and has refused to surrender. We all know what the Jerries are like. They will not give up a place without a fight and they are well fortified in these islands. There are a few small boats that have escaped this month with local men, some having reached France and some unfortunate ones who were picked up off the Islands are now in prison.'

8th October to 12th November. 'There was an American plane knocked down at Bouley Bay on October 31st. It was fully lit up and was distinct but the blighters here must have thought it grand to bring down a helpless plane. Only the pilot was saved. The fuel and food problem is getting worse as each week passes. The sugar for adults will stop next week. The ration was only 2 ounces and no more salt. Everything is in a critical state. No leather for shoe repairs and no boots or shoes available or clothing which is very scarce. People get what they can from second hand shops.'

November 1944. 'We have had a Red Letter day, the importance of which cannot be realized, but only by those who suffer like ourselves in these Islands and have undergone what we have in the last 4½ years, especially since the Invasion last June when our Islands have had to rely mostly on what they can produce, which does not cover a great number of essential things for our welfare. So today has brought joy to our hearts to hear of a Red Cross relief boat having been promised us with medical supplies, soap and food parcels. We do nothing but plan for that great day when our share will be in our possession.

Monica has chicken pox but not very severe. Had the doctor to try to have extra milk or something. The doctor tried but it was rejected but she had ¼ pound cocoa for four weeks.'

'On December 7th we heard the good news that our boat was due to leave Lisbon today enroute for Guernsey and then to Jersey. Roy has developed chicken pox and seems to have it rather severe.'

25th December, Christmas Day. 'A quiet one. But for the children's sake we made the best of it. They had very little in their stockings: a tennis ball each, dominoes for Roy, dolls clothes for Monica and each a book, but they were delighted as in these days they get so little toys that it is not hard to please them.'

Good for our Morale

Entertaining at home, listening to popular music, going to the cinema, enjoying a snide swipe at the Germans, supporting amateur shows, all helped to pass the time and keep up the spirits of those who had to endure so much hardship during the Occupation.

'People weren't living like vegetables. There was a lot going on, in fact.'

'We used to entertain as usual, but our guests brought their own bread and butter, sometimes cakes.'

11th September. 'I went with the children to George and Valerie for the weekend at St. Mary's. We had a real good time especially as we had not to bring any food. They gave us a real treat of white bread and farm butter. They are more fortunate than we are that they get a few extras from the farm.'

'I can remember – about 1943 or 44 – an all night party in the country. We went to a dance at one of the Parish Halls. It ended before curfew, then we all went to a farm. There we had a fantastic meal of pork and roast potatoes, followed by dancing and games. A wonderful night!'

'The 'Bagot Bashers' used to have a dance every two weeks at Sion Hall where the L'Emeraude Hotel now is.'

'The two main dancing spots in town were the Plaza and the Chelsea Hotel where most of the clubs held their dances.'

Autumn 1940. 'The dance at West Park Pavilion last evening was again well attended and went off splendidly. It is estimated there were about 450 present, including a large number of German officers, NCO's and men, among whom were the Island Commandant, the Air Commandant and the Harbour Commandant, who seemed to take a keen and active interest in the proceedings. Music was by Syd Britton's Band, . . . the closing down hour at 10 o'clock.'

Once wirelesses had been confiscated in June 1942, music lovers had to be content with listening to what they already had on record or on sheet music.

'On Sunday nights one of us would read to the rest of the family by the light of the fire, then we would listen to the gramophone while we played a game of Bezique.'

'The piano came into its own and at home we used to have sing songs round it.'

'Our favourite tunes were all pre-war. They included *Smoke Gets In Your Eyes, Red Sails in the Sunset, Look for the Silver Lining*, and *Bless This House*. We also liked *Run Rabbit Run Rabbit, Roll out the Barrel*, and specially anything by Ivor Novello.'

'Leyton and Johnstone were very popular. I can remember *Bye, Bye, Black Bird* being a great favourite.'

WESTS CINEMA

TO-DAY
AND TO-MORROW
at 6.30 only

~~~~~~

A ROBINSON

A marvellous picture of
amazing adventure in German

Also "DANZIG" a film of
great interest—and
LONDON'S ORDEAL in the News

NOTICE

FOR German films with
English sub-titles
the left-hand section of
the stalls are reserved
for <u>Civilians only</u>; the
right-hand section and
the Balcony for German
troops only.

Left: German films shown
at Wests Cinema, St
Helier

'When I went to England after the war I felt quite out of it. I didn't know any of the latest songs or the characters in Tommy Handley's *Itma*.'

Music from an unexpected source came from the Germans themselves. Not only did they always sing on the march but they also arranged military band concerts. One of the first was performed by the German Air Force Band in the Royal Parade.

'When the Germans first arrived the response to their concerts was cool but afterwards people listened to them.'

Then there was the German 'travelling' Orchestra. One of their concerts, which included Schubert's *Unfinished Symphony* and Mozart's *Kleine Nachtmusik*, provoked two letters of appreciation in the *Evening Post's* letter column – both signed *Music Lover*.

'The tune I best remember is the one the Germans used to march to – *Ie Io*. We used to hum it and whistle it. It was almost like their National Anthem.'

Cinemas of that time, with their cafés, were great social centres as well as being places where films were shown. There were dances in the Forum's Golden Lounge, concerts of popular music on their Compton organ, even 'Community Singing on Sundays (when circumstances permit)'.

Though there was a scheme for Guernsey and Jersey to swap whatever British films they still had, German films became the main feature of Occupation cinema programmes. So a notice was put out to segregate the Occupier from the Occupied. 'For German films with English sub-titles the left hand section of the stalls are reserved for civilians only; the right hand section and the balcony for German troops only.'

6th August. 'The town was swarming with German soldiers. Also at the pictures. (We now have German pictures and news.)'

But sometimes the civilians in the audience were too vociferous in their response to what they were watching and the Germans issued an order banning 'Cinema demonstrations'. This was, however, modified to the extent that, though whistling was still 'verboten', 'you may applaud comedians or heroes'.

And there was always writing and reading. The July 1940 *Islander* encouraged the writing:

'Some of our regular contributors have left Jersey, but there is, we know, a wealth of hidden talent in the Island.

If you will co-operate with us – send us your ideas, stories, articles, agricultural advice, economy tricks and household hints at once – we will give you the finest paper of local talent that Jersey has yet seen.'

The swastika-emblazoned Forum, St Helier, showing the German film
'Victory in the West'

Lack of paper, however, meant that the *Islander* sadly did not appear again after March 1941.

There were other outlets for talent, though, and one of these was to write a verse or two on a topical subject and get it published. Reg Grandin was a dab hand at it and in June 1943 he contributed to the 'Great Jam Controversy' which he explains:

'The Jam Ration was distributed at stated intervals and alphabetically. Some people complained that, owing to the first letter of their surname occurring towards the end of the alphabet, they always received the dregs and pips from the bottom of the kegs.

The surname that my parents bore,
Quite suited me before the War,
But since they've issued ration jam,
A discontented soul I am.

I do not ask for Marmalade.
Or Jam that's labelled 'Jersey Maid';
But, when it's ladled out from kegs.
Why should I always have the dregs?

I do not think the fault is mine,
That when my signature I sign,
The name of YORRICK stands revealed,
Instead of Amy, Dobbs or Field.'

Another popular form for writers was that of the short story. Winter Le Brocq and V. J. Bailhache were just two who used it to comment on the times they were living through. In *A Tin of Salmon*, Bailhache takes a light hearted look at bartering. Aunt Jemima's Christmas present to her nephew Tom – 'There's nothing I like better than salmon' – was exchanged for a pair of stockings, ten cigars, a second-hand hat and finally Aunt Jemima's shawl. In exchange, you've guessed it, the aunt receives back her tin of salmon.

Le Brocq's *The Obliging Kommandant* is in much more sombre mood. The theme is the brutality of the Germans to their Russian 'slave' workers. Two elderly sisters are horrified to see from their back window two German guards flogging a Russian. The younger of the two sisters decides to walk into town to see the Kommandant. 'We felt you would do something – do something quickly,' she explains. The Kommandant does. When the two sisters wake up next morning they wonder why no light is coming through their back windows. 'The two old ladies stepped out to the garden. All the windows at the back and on the sides of the villa had been boarded up during the night and the boards bore the seal of the obliging Kommandant!'

Specially good reading for Jersey people who still spoke Jersey Norman French, the Island's own language, was the series started by *Les Chroniques de Jersey*. This French newspaper printed in St. Helier, on 31st August 1940, published the first of their *Brachie d'Histouethes en Jerriais*. These were introduced to readers, in French, as a way of pleasing all those who still spoke the 'vierr parler' and in memory of their author, PL Le Sueur Mourant. Amusingly the series also caused a fortnight's suspension by the Germans of *Les Chroniques*, while a copy was sent to Paris for the Jersey-French to be deciphered!

This unintelligibility of Jersey Norman French to non-Islanders, by the by, led to its unexpected revival in the Occupation. It gave great joy to its speakers that it could be used with impunity, even in buses or shops crowded with Germans. The language served both as a link with Jersey's independent past and as a special bond between Islanders of true Jersey stock.

Perhaps the best remembered entertainment of this period, though, was that put on by various amateur groups. One was the Little Choir who gave 'rare entertainment' round the Parish Halls; another the Log Cabin Boys – signature tune *She'll be Coming Round the Mountain* – who featured in shows at the Opera House. Names associated with the musical side of shows were Lyndon Marguerie, orchestral conductor for *Mount Parnasse*, and PG Larbalestier, composer of *Les Paladins*. The well known actor Terence Dudley, who was here in the Occupation, acted under the name of Paul Williams. Richard Whinnerah and Kenneth Britton collaborated to put on many of the shows.

Madeleine Le Riche was one of the main choreographers and supplier of dancers from her dancing school. Looking back now to the shows that were put on every fortnight she says, 'It's amazing what we were able to do. For a Scottish number, for instance, everybody somehow found a kilt and wore a black velvet jacket, even if the jacket was made from curtains'.

Other details from that time that Madeleine Le Riche remembers were the German requests:

'The Commandant had to have a translation of everything in triplicate, even if the lyric were only "Oh dear, what can the matter be!" When the Bailiff's own interpretor, a German speaking Jerseyman, translated a nursery rhyme to be sung by the children, the Commandant commented that it was the best translation he had seen so far.

Then there was the time when the day before the show I was asked to keep the first row of the Dress Circle free for the Commandant on the first night. He didn't come. I was asked to do the same for the following night. He didn't come then either. It was just to keep us on our toes!

We used to take part of our shows, or sometimes the whole show, out to the Parish Halls. It was a great outing for us. And they always laid on something special for us to eat.'

'Getting to and from rehearsals in the blackout was the problem. I lived at Cleveland Road and I can remember once trying to find my way down Hill Street to Halkett Place. I walked in the middle of the road and tried to guide my way by the stars but when I thought I was turning into Halkett Place, I bumped up against a brick wall.'

'We hear that the residents of Kensington Place have now discovered that the incessant rat-tat which disturbs their slumbers is not due to nocturnal machine gun practice. Mr Winter Le Brocq, still on the heights of Montparnasse, has written since that production, three new plays.'

The audiences too look back on the Opera House shows with pleasure.

'We had permanent bookings. It was a great thrill to go. Even though the Opera House wasn't heated there was a full house from Monday to Saturday.'

'Kenneth Britton's "Revue" was wonderful. The chorus wore white sheets beautifully cut, with buttons all down the back.'

Tuesday, 11th August 1942. 'Have been to Opera House to see *Hullo Again*, a revue, and one of the few which I have really enjoyed. The house was absolutely packed, chairs down the aisles and people standing. They did some excerpts from *Lilac Time*. There was one scene which was very cleverly done. It was a "black out" scene with the costumes and even rims of spectacles outlined in light. There was a flower woman at the back and all the flowers lit up. It was arranged by the Electricity Co. and I am told that the Germans have been to enquire how it was done as they said they had never seen anything like it in Germany or anywhere else. Aren't we just clever! Two Germans were standing at the back for some time, I wondered if they just came in to hear *Lilac Time*.'

'It was good for our morale to have those things to go to.'

Only one sour note, and with hindsight a sinister one too, was struck in the German reception of Jersey's amateur shows. The author of the suspect show? None other than William Shakespeare, as Grandin relates:

'In December, 1943, at the Opera House, the Jersey Green Room Club presented *The Merchant of Venice*. After the first night's performance, the actor who was taking the part of Shylock was summoned to German Head-Quarters. There he was informed that his delineation of the character of the Jew was not considered sufficiently repellent, and that

94

Jersey Theatre programme, 1944

this would have to be remedied at subsequent performances, or further measures would be taken!'

We would add that this diatribe (with its accompanying threat) was completely ignored by the actor concerned, Mr Richard Whinnerah.

The following is an imagined account of this interview, incorporating the reply that the actor would, no doubt, have liked to have been able to make!

The German Official
What tidings hath this moment reached mine ears?
That thou, in William Shakespeare's famous Play,
The wicked Jew didst make an object of men's pity,
And, on far kindlier lines than those we own
His venom'd character did thus portray:
See to it then on subsequent occasion
The Jew is pictured as devoid of soul
Fail not in this, lest consequence dread
Attend thy heedlessness!

The Actor
To thy inglorious discourse have I listened,
Fill'd with the biased views of all thy race,
From Attila, the Hun, thy blood is tinctured,
And bowels of compassion hast thou none!
I did but draw the Jew within the limits
Of human charity, as taught to all:
But thy vile creed its cruel demands pursueth,
The pound of flesh and, after that, the blood
Of this unhappy, persecuted race:
Who then is greater villain?
He who stays his hand, by this appalled,
That his revenge should thus two deaths encompass?
Or he who thousands slay, for little cause
Save blind unreason?
Go! Ponder well fair Portia's noble words,
'The quality of Mercy is not strained,'
Which also to the hunted Jew doth well apply:
Then answer give, and, if thy conscience be not dead,
Thou'lt no more seek to change, in slightest measure,
The presentation of the Jew I've made!

Them and Us

'One never feels really at ease anywhere' – sums up the pervading atmosphere engendered by the German presence in Jersey. What were they going to do next? For the majority of Islanders, however, that fear, flamed by rumour, was far worse than anything that actually befell them.

'Things that never happened were the worst feature of the Occupation. You knew someone who knew someone who worked for the Commandant who had said that on Tuesday all the men of military age were going to be deported. When it didn't happen on Tuesday, well, it would be on Friday. If it wasn't this Friday, it would be next Friday. And so on.'

The majority of the German troops here wanted to co-exist peacefully with the Islanders. Many of them were not committed members of the Nazi party – they even tried to shield Jersey from the worst effects of Hitler's totalitarian commands. Before the Order to confiscate all wireless sets was confirmed in June 1942, the German authorities here had themselves gone to Paris in an effort to get the Order rescinded. Jersey, with no fighting or bombing, was considered a good posting and, on the whole, the troops responded by being as pleasant as possible.

'One couldn't fault their behaviour' was a general feeling. Many were impressed by the way the troops adhered to the 'terribly severe discipline' they were put under. Their singing as they marched was not spontaneous, they had to sing. The hold that officers had over their men stood one erring Jerseyman in good stead. 'My wife and I were sunbathing on a 'verboten' beach when some Germans came along. As they passed they saluted me – they thought I was a German officer with his Jersey girl friend!'

Drunkenness was looked on with disfavour and a boy at that time remembers one occasion when it was peremptorily dealt with: a crowd of rowdily tipsy Germans were turfed off the No. 9 double decker going from town back to St. Ouen by their own military police.

There was, though, one occasion which the Feldgendarmerie were not there to see. Some Germans, who had been enjoying a drink in the Victoria Hotel, suddenly spotted the porcelain figure of a stout man, wrapped round in his cloak, advertising 'Sandeman'. Immediately one of them seized it, gleefully shouted 'Churchill, Churchill' and ran off with it down Minden Place, angrily chased by the landlord.

Even excusable behaviour of his own countrymen was immediately checked by Jersey's first Commandant. After the austerity of Germany, the goods-filled shops ready for the tourists of 1940, were a temptation for the troops that they could not resist. But Gussek, the first Commandant, put a stop to this frenzied buying just over a week after the Occupation began.

Order of the Commandant of the German Troops in Occupation of Jersey

Important Notice

Shopkeepers of the Island of Jersey are notified that I have informed the members of the German Forces in the Island they must not purchase more than:

50 cigarettes or 25 cigars;
1 bottle of wine or 2 bottles of beer to take away for their own consumption;
3 shirts, collars, and ties;
Only one suit length of cloth allowed per man.

All purchases must be restricted in quantity as above.

In the event of a larger quantity being required, an order will be issued by myself.

No foodstuffs, other than fruit, biscuits, confectionery, may be bought by any soldier.

In case of doubt, the matter must be referred to the Commandant, who will give a decision.

(signed) GUSSEK, Hauptmann,
German Commandant of the Island of Jersey

If their own troops had to obey orders, then the Islanders were expected to do so as well. As new Orders seemed to be issued daily, so infringements of them happened daily too. An offending Islander would appear before one of two main courts according to who had caught him. A charge by one of Jersey's own policemen would be heard by the Island's magistrate. A charge by one of the German police, the Feldgendarmerie or the un-uniformed Gestapo, would be heard at the Commandant's court. The German punishments ranged from a summons to College House or one of the other German Headquarters, to imprisonment. The worst punishment – deportation – will be looked at in a following chapter.

Amongst the petty crimes that were punished were riding two abreast (the cycles were sometimes confiscated); sneering at a German; throwing manure at a column of troops (the young lady had the original sentence of three months imprisonment doubled on appeal!). A typical case of this nature, though more lightly dealt with, involved Mrs Florence Carter, proprietress of a newsagent in Colomberie. She was crossing over the road near her shop when she was knocked down by a German car. She was taken to hospital with leg injuries and while she was there she was tried, by the Feldgendarmerie and the Honorary police. Their findings were that she had been at fault – for jaywalking. She was fined an initial 10 Reichsmarks, with a further 5 marks for every day that the fine remained unpaid. She did not appeal because she admitted to her family, 'I crossed over without looking where I was going'.

The Feldgendarmerie, 'Chain Gain', or 'dog collars', so called because of the chain they wore around their necks, were naturally not popular as a group. They were rather shot-happy with their pistols too:

'All lights are supposed to be out at 11 p.m. I didn't think mine could be seen from the road, I was still reading at 11.55 last night and had a bad fright when I heard footsteps in the road at the side of the house, then a pistol shot, then footsteps along Colomberie and then another pistol shot right outside the house. Out went my light, but I still have it lit tonight at 11.30.'

The German equivalent of the Naafi at the back of the Mayfair Hotel, St Saviour's Road, St Helier

Even the Felgendarmerie, however, were not consistent in their approach to their duty. 'They commandeered a neighbour's car, but they didn't touch ours.' It seemed that some Germans allowed some Islanders more latitude than others, as is exemplified by this typical tale of two neighbours:

'One day my neighbour said, "I've got a piece of black market indoors but it's too big for me. Would you like half?" "I'll come and have a look at it" I said. It was a piece of beef, so I said I'd have half. Then we got chatting and before we knew it, it was after curfew. So I came out of her house with the beef and crossed the road. I opened my door and said to my husband who was standing there, "What are you standing in the dark for?" he said. "Put the light out quick, old —'s dog's barking like hell, the *dog collars* must be around." Then there was a bang, bang on the door. Now our lights should have been out. So I pushed the beef into the kitchen cupboard, shut the kitchen door, and told my husband to stay where he was as I, being a woman, could deal with the Jerries best.

When I opened the door there were two on the doorstep. "You have your light on, Madam." "I just switched it on to see the time, we have no Big Ben now to tell us the time. I am just going to bed." They let me off. But next day my neighbour came to me to say they'd been to her house too, because they'd got the light on as well. Her husband opened the door and said the light came from a candle. One of the Germans reached up and touched the light bulb – it was still hot. So her husband wasn't only fined for having the light on after hours but for telling a lie as well. That wasn't all. As my neighbour's husband and the Jerries were talking at the front door, the cat they were looking after for somebody who'd been evacuated to England, shot out. The man dashed out after it. He was then fined for being out after curfew.'

It was risky, as we have seen, to appeal against a conviction. Some were lucky and had their fine or sentence reduced: others had it doubled. 'You could never be sure if they were going to be for you or against you.'

On occasion, though, the Germans listened to reason, they were even humane. When they wanted to re-open the Eastern Railway to facilitate the movement of military goods and personnel, the Hambie family received a demolition order for their home in Marina Avenue. The house had been built on former railway land and it had to go if the trains were to run from St. Helier to Gorey once more. Nevertheless, the order was eventually rescinded. The Germans had been persuaded to run the track down by the side of the house instead of through it.

Again, although processions were banned, on every 11th November during the Occupation, wreaths in remembrance of those who had died in the first British/German war could be placed on the

The former Colliers shop in St Helier, taken over by the Germans as a shop selling German publications

cenotaph. When two British airmen, whose bodies were washed up on the coast of La Pulente and La Marie in 1943, were allowed a military funeral, the Germans showed great tact. With the funeral arranged for Sunday, 'at 10 p.m. Saturday evening the German authorities informed the undertakers (Mr J. B. Le Quesne) that it had been decided that the people of Jersey would feel better if as few of their troops attended the funeral as possible, therefore they would provide only a firing party and bearers. The service was to be conducted by the Dean of Jersey'.

Jersey women, particularly after hearing the tales brought over

Jersey cream ices in Charing Cross, St Helier tempted German soldiers too

from Occupied France, were quite surprised at the respect they were shown by their Occupiers. 'My sister and I often came home late from the theatre but not once did they even speak to us.'

Wednesday, 15th April 1942. 'Have been to see *The Pirates of Penzance* this evening, it was very good. Forgot all about closing the greenhouse until nearly curfew (10 o'clock). I rushed down Roseville Street and on the way back met crowds of Germans coming from the Forum. Father had got worried and had started off to meet me but though I was practically the only civilian about, nobody said a word to me. A couple of years ago the thought of being out alone with hundreds of Germans in the street would have been petrifying to say the least.'

The Germans, on their side, tried many times to win over the Islanders. They arranged band and sacred concerts to which they invited the general public. The first football match they organised was played in Victoria College field as early as 19th August, 1940. On that occasion the score was Jersey XI 4, the German team 6.

Neither did the Occupiers miss an opportunity to put over their side of the story. As well as German films, the German news was always shown at the cinemas. As early as 15th December, 1940, German periodicals were introduced into St. Helier's Public Library. 25,000-word German-English-German dictionaries 'with dialogues, etc.,' were on sale at all leading newsagents.

What the purpose of the following incident was, though, Mr Le Moignan is uncertain of to this day. The Bouley Bay Hotel, now demolished, had been taken over by German troops and one day, as a young telephone engineer apprentice, Mr Le Moignan was called out, ostensibly to repair a fault at the hotel.

Mr Le Moignan recalls that he was taken by three Germans in a car not directly there but by a roundabout route which included Rozel Bay. On his arrival, he was invited into the bar, where he was immediately struck by a huge mural on one of the walls – a hand-painted pin-up picture of a woman in tights and skimpy dress.

It was the first time, he says, that he had seen such a thing.

He was invited to have a drink at the bar with the men, whom he remembers were from the German Air Force, but mindful of the risk of being labelled a collaborator, he refused.

Finally, he was taken back to the telephone workers in town without having been asked to put right the fault he had been called to rectify.

There are all sorts of possible explanations for this unusual moment in his life, but Mr Le Moignan wonders whether it may have been to get a young and impressionable man in a vitally important trade on the side of the Occupying forces.

Individually, the courtesy of the Germans was their hallmark:

'We played tennis last night and I sent a ball over into a patch of potatoes and two Germans went looking for it for me!'

'It was a very blustery day, with an easterly wind blowing down Kensington Place where we were walking along with a friend. Ahead of us were two soldiers. Suddenly a gust blew off my friend's trilby and it sailed along in the gutter towards the sea, passing the two Germans. One of them retrieved the hat, looked round and gave it back to my friend. There was a feeling of camaraderie in that small incident.'

Monday, 13th July. 'Went to church y'day morning. Was wearing a navy flower on a white jacket (made out of part a linen sheet at least a hundred years old!) Felt something fall at my feet. A German officer was passing in a car, he slowed up and called out in English, "You have dropped something". Hardly one's pre-occupation idea of what the Nazis were like!'

'I wondered this morning what my friends would have thought if they could have seen me all alone in the house with a German soldier. He had only come to pay an account and was most polite, but looked a typical German, the kind you see caricatured, round head, blue eyes beaming through spectacles. He was dying to shake hands but I didn't give him the chance, so he clicked his heels and departed.'

Then, as with most soldiers, there was their love of children.

'I was walking at Havre des Pas when a German bent over the pram and picked up my baby. I was terrified.'

'My little boy was playing in the Park on Mount Bingham when a soldier gave him an orange. He'd never seen an orange before so he didn't know what to do with it. When he brought it home I had a good look at it to make sure it hadn't been tampered with. When I saw it was O.K. I allowed him to eat it.'

'Our daughter was out in the garden in the pram and we came across this rather older officer talking to her and being pleasant with her. We went up to him. In German he made us understand that he was very interested in the child, that he had children of his own and he started producing photographs. It was very clear that he was looking for the day when he would be no longer in Jersey but back with his family.'

'On the way to school we used to call in at the German bakehouse in Charles Street. They used to give us a bag of bread ends – the trimmings off their loaves of black bread. I liked it.'

'My father was a milkman and used to deliver to the German H.Q. at La Garrenne. When I went with him and took the milk into the kitchen, I was always given a real biscuit, not the rock hard ones we were used to.'

'The Todt Organisation had built a railway almost following the old Jersey Eastern track. The train had a diesel engine and small trucks and they used to get sand from near Gorey village and then bring it back towards town to make concrete. One or two of the drivers used to give a

A sign by the church in St Helier points to German Headquarters in Victoria College House, Bagatelle Road

toot as they passed our school at the end of the afternoon and I can remember jumping onto the sand trucks as far as La Rocque and then jumping off again.'

Kindness was sometimes shown to adults, though, as well.

'I used to go with two buckets to West Park slip to collect sea water. Many people did. When the guard at the slip saw the people standing in front of the Grand Hotel waiting to cross, he would keep his back turned on purpose to allow people to fill their buckets.'

'As my wife was pregnant, I cycled into the country to get some skimmed milk and two eggs. On my way back, I was stopped by the German patrol and told to take off my knapsack and empty my pockets. When I told them that the milk and eggs were for my pregnant wife, they took a sympathic view and let me go. It was a good thing they didn't search me any further, because I had my trousers tucked into my socks, and where the two met, my crystal set was resting!'

Two Germans who left pleasant memories behind are one who was billeted in the same house that a family were looking after for someone else, and one who had the nick-name of Crabbio. Of the billetee: 'He turned out to be a very pleasant young fellow. He spoke excellent French, so we were able to communicate with him. One of the amusing things that he said on one occasion in the gloriously fine summer we had, the second summer of the war, while he was lolling in a deck chair in bathing trunks, was 'how absurd the whole thing was. He was being paid an extra mark a day for being at the front!'.

The second was one of the Germans down at St. Helier Harbour. He was always asking the fishermen if they had got a crab for him – hence his nickname Crabbio. 'He used to turn a blind eye if the fishermen took more fish for themselves than they should.'

The well-known love of music that Germans have, provided one or two lighter moments for Islanders:

April, 1942. 'Mrs Struthers told me today that the German Lutheran Padre who lives quite close to the Manse went to ask if he could use the telephone. He said he had been to the performance of *The Messiah* and had enjoyed it very much. He asked Mr Struthers if Handel wrote it in Germany, and when told he had written it in England, the Padre looked quite fed up.'

Another time a lady was practising Chopin on her piano, when she was aware from the reflection in the picture in front of her that somebody was listening at the window. It was a German. Then she heard him knock on the door. He asked her in broken English whether he might play on her piano. She replied that he could certainly play on her piano – when the war was over, but not before!

Those at the top of the German hierarchy of command had their public image too. There seems to have been real co-operation between the Island's first Commandant Gussek and the Jersey authorities. According to the Bailiff, Coutanche, 'Gussek was perfectly happy to let civil administration continue under his (Coutanche's) control'.

'I went to tennis this evening and heard why Mrs Mackintosh (a chiropodist) could not come last week. She had been summoned to Government House to attend to Gussek's toes! She said he was very nice, we have heard he is, and was dressed ready for a game of tennis. He now speaks a few words of English. She told him she came from Scotland, but he apparently had never heard of such a place!'

Of his successor, Schumacher, rumour had it that he 'had been obliged to resign for being too lenient', while his replacement Knackfuss had the reputation of being 'a real Hun!'.

Lower down the pyramid of control, Leslie Sinel notes in his diary after six months of Occupation, one exception to his impression that 'there is little arrogance among the enemy'. He names him as a Lieutenant Schnor, 'perhaps the only one who has gone out of his way to be grossly annoying, and he is not popular even among his brother officers'.

There was then a real dilemma for many people as to how the Germans were to be treated. The following story exemplifies one aspect:

'I woke up with a jerk, why, I did not know (later I knew the answer). It was pitch black as the curtains were closed because of the blackout – I think the time was about 2 or 3 in the morning – then I suddenly heard footsteps above me in the roof space, I cannot call it a loft or attic because there was no access to it from the house. The steps then travelled from above my room into my parents'. By this time I had awakened my parents and they, at first disbelieving me, also heard the noise above.

The steps then stopped and all was quiet. About ten minutes later, I cannot remember the exact time, the sound of snoring was heard. Yelling out brought forth no reply and then we were in a dilemma – was it an English parachutist who had landed on the roof – or what? It took a long time to make up our minds what to do, but eventually from outside, right on cue, a German cycle patrol came along, so we called out to them. When they arrived and asked what the noise was about, we explained that someone was on the roof. At first they would not believe us – even after clambering up on the roof of adjoining outbuildings. My father insisted that they get up on to the roof and provided the steps for them to do that. There was then jubilation on their part when they discovered that the tiles of the roof had been stripped off making a hole. They then went inside, one of them in the process putting his foot through the ceiling – right above my head!

When they eventually emerged, thankfully it was not an Englishman, but apparently a German deserter. And off they went.

The next morning we received a call from some officers who "thanked" us for reporting the finding of a deserter – and that was the last we heard of the incident.

To this day, we still wonder if we were right in calling in the patrol – what *would* we have done if it *had* been an English parachutist?'

The whole 'them' and 'us' relationship can perhaps best be summed up in these comments:

GERMAN-ENGLISH CONVERSATION

DEUTSCH
GERMAN

ENGLISCH
ENGLISH

Deutsch German	engl. Aussprache der deutschen Woerter / Engl. pronunciation of German words	Englisch English	German pronunciation of English words / dɔ :tsche Aussprache der engl. Woerter
Aofahrt	ab'-fahrt	departure	dipart'schoer
abladen	ab'-lah-den	unload	anlohd
Anfang	an'-fahng	beginning	beginning
Armee	ahr-mai'	army	armie
aufstellen	ouf'-sta-len	draw up	droh ap
auskleiden	ous-kly-den	undress	andress
Baum	boum	tree	trie
bei	by	near	niehr
beladen	ba-lah'-den	load	lohd
beobachten	ba-o'-bah-ten	observe	obsoerf
es ist schade	as est shah'-de	it is a pity	it is e pittie
das macht nichts	das mah't nix	narrow mind	nerroh meind
nicht so schnell	neeh't so shnall	not so quickly	not so kwicklie
selbstverständlich	salbst'var-stand-lik	of course	of korss
im Gegenteil	im gai'-gen-tyl	on the contrary	on se Kon'trerie
unterwegs	oon-tar-waix'	on the way	on se weh
plötzlich	pluts'-lik	suddenly	saddenlie
das ist Unsinn	das est oon'-sen	that is nonsense	set is nonsenss
das ist zu viel	das est tsoo feel	that is too much	sat is tuh matsch
warten Sie auf mich	wahr-ten zee ouf mik	wait for me	weht for mie
ein en Augenblick	yn ou'-gen-blick	a moment	a moment

'I was escorted up to the inner door by a German who came in after me. He tried to be nice and gave me a beaming smile when he found I didn't understand what he was saying. That is the worst of it, individually some of them are very nice and it seems impossible not to be polite, but collectively one hates them all.'

'The Germans, for the most part, seem to be out to make a good impression and there is no doubt that they respect the local population . . . Germans mingle with the people on the pavements, but we just look through them as if they were not there.'

'When Madeleine got on a bus this afternoon, it was packed and a German got up and gave her a seat. In most cases they are very polite, but complain that we ignore them.'

'Altogether we thought we were being very leniently treated and appreciated the fact.'

'The Germans would hold their service in the town church on a Sunday morning an hour before we did. They would bring their own altar ornaments and come and go very quietly without any fuss. It didn't make sense that we should be using the same church, praying to the same God – and be at war with each other.'

Defiance

Rebellion against the Germans, on the scale of the organised resistance in Occupied Europe during the war, would have been impossible in a fortified island the size of Jersey. It would also have been counter to the wishes of the Jersey authorities themselves. They believed that the safest way to alleviate the effect of the German presence in the Island was to obey German orders.

Major Rybot's 1d. stamp —
note the 'A' in each corner

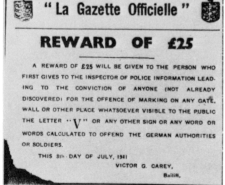

La Gazette Officielle notice,
July 1941

The defiant V sign at the corner of Undercliffe and Queen's Road, only yards away from the German Headquarters of Infantry Regiment 582, in Gloucester House Hotel, St Helier

The Jerseyman, though, is noted for his stubborn and independent nature. He found many subtle ways, therefore, to show he was still his own man. Two of the best examples of this concern Jersey's issue of its own stamps. Their first designer, Major Rybot, managed, despite the Commandant's scrutiny, to incorporate the English Royal Shield, an A in the corners of the 1d. stamp and two As and two Bs to fill the four corners of the ½d. stamp. Only after the Occupation did Islanders learn that the four A's stood for 'Ad Avernum Adolf Atrox' – 'to hell with Atrocious Adolf' and the substitution of the two B's on the ½d. sent Italy's dictator, 'Bloody Benito', to the same place too. And the Germans rushed to buy them!

Tuesday, 1st April. 'Today was the first day of issue of our new postage stamps and everybody seems to have been busy posting themselves letters. I was told Germans were at the G.P.O. before it opened, bought 1,500, stuck them on envelopes, had them date stamped and they were on sale in Berlin in the afternoon. The Commandant is reported to have bought £50 worth. They are 1d. stamps, red, and bear the Jersey Coat of Arms, very much the same as the Guernsey ones which were issued.'

Edmund Blampied in 1943 incorporated a GR (George Rex) motif in his set. This even went as far as Paris to be printed without one German spotting the act of defiance.

More controversial was the V for Victory campaign which Colonel Britain encouraged all Occupied countries to mount:

'The scheme seems to be to present the "V" in some way or another and whenever you can and so eventually force the Germans to realise that everybody is against them. "V" in morse code is ...–. This can be heard in the opening notes of Beethoven's V (5th) Symphony. When knocking on a door give three sharp raps and one long one, when you want to attract a person's attention in a restaurant or in the street tap it out or whistle it, salute everybody with the "V" sign made with your fingers, or paint them whenever you can, scratch it on their cars and lorries, in fact cover your world with "V"s.

This fellow speaks so well that you want to dash out and start doing it right away.'

And many Islanders did. It seemed an ideal way to relieve their frustrated feelings of oppression.

Saturday, 28th June 1941. 'Heard on the wireless some encouragement concerning the V for victory which thrills me but I'm afraid that little can be done yet here though we can all beat out the V in many ways.'

But who exactly commemorated the first anniversary of the Occupation with them is not known. The German reaction though was immediate.

Tuesday, 1st July. 'One year ago. Surely we shall not have to say "Two years ago". Several of the German Notice Boards have been inscribed with "Britain will win" and similar words, also large V's, so warning in Evening Post tonight that unless the guilty person confesses before the 3rd, first the district concerned will have to provide a civil guard at night; second, all wireless sets in the district will be confiscated, and third, the district will be fined.'

Sunday, 20th July 1941. 'There is great excitement in this house today for it is the great day of mobilising the V's. We stayed up till midnight last night to hear Colonel Britain on the wireless, Mother and I sitting up with a flicker of a light on the electric as the electric must not be used after 11 p.m.'

So the signs continued to appear, and eventually the Croad household suffered as a result of the reprisal.

Saturday, 25th October. 'V-signs having been put up in several districts, including this one, male members of the population between the ages of 18 and 55 have to provide a civil guard at night and wireless sets are confiscated including ours of course. Policeman arrived this evening to warn brother that he would be fetched at 1.30 a.m. on Monday. Feel awful at losing wireless set.'

The punishment was bad enough when it affected the whole district where the V signs were found. It was much worse for the culprits themselves.

Sunday, 27th July 1941. 'We have heard some distressing news concerning two young women in this island, one of these being married with a small baby. They were two sisters out for a walk and happened to come across a V on the road. They picked it up and are supposed to have put it against a German sign board. But within seconds some Germans were around them and arrested them, and from then they never returned to their homes and were sent off to Germany today for nine months. It has been deeply felt by all of us to think that for such a small crime these women have to be so brutally dealt with.'

It is no wonder then that Bernard Baker debated the rightness of the whole V sign campaign in Jersey in the pages of his diary.

'The point is, "Is it worth it". Do we achieve anything doing these things? Apparently the BBC in its broadcast this last week has been praising and acclaiming the peoples of the occupied countries for perpetrating these petty signs of revolt, but tell me, what possible good can it do? What possible harm can it do to the enemy war machine? None whatsoever of course, but it does give the German the opportunity to pounce down on a defenceless people and by punishing them show them who is the master, however temporary he may be.'

He continued to ponder the whole question of sabotage.

'I should like to be guided as to the best way to damage the German war machine. I can of course kill a German, sabotage an aeroplane, destroy a number of lorries and possibly in some way or another sink a ship, but if by so doing I bring heavy punishments to bear on 40,000 people (mind I am speaking of Jersey only, not of occupied France, Holland, etc. for possibly the same conditions could not exist there) and possibly be the cause of sending many able bodied people to slave in Germany's factories, am I a "patriot?" or am I a "traitor?", the question is not so easy to answer as might appear.'

The German answer to the V campaign was to adopt it themselves:

'Last Thursday (17th July) "V"s' suddenly put in an appearance on all houses and buildings occupied by the Germans, and to our consternation it is not difficult to see that the culprit this time is no other than our old friend "The Boche". Further all cars and lorries carry the "V"; the only difference between the "V" for victory and the "V" for "vernichtung" which I understand means disaster or annihilation is that the German "V" is surrounded by laurel leaves. The great people are just surrounding themselves with them in an effort to ridicule the campaign. I wonder if

112

they realise just what an admission this is on their part that the "V" is getting them down. Really, when the "V" battle just put in an appearance on the Jersey front, I must admit that I thought it was being a great deal over-rated, but, gosh damn it, can you imagine the British people allowing themselves to be so absolutely intimidated by such a campaign and in any case, in so short a time, because after all, it is only in the last two or three months that the "V" has really got going. Yesterday, enrolment day for the "V" army, saw quite a number of "V"s put in various places around the island. A flight of some twenty steps leading to the upper gardens at Westmount (and quite a favourite spot with the Huns) had "V" on every step. "V"s were painted in the roadway at Mont au Prêtre and chalked up in several other places in the town. I am sure that the German "V" will not stop the "V" battle, rather will it have the opposite effect: for now it has become almost a duty to "V" in some way or another. You can hear cyclists doing it on their bells, the telephone rings – three sharp rings and a long one, door bells and knockers suffer from the same malady, and the "V" greeting is becoming more and more common. That such a childish thing should have come to mean so much is really one of the remarkable things in this "crazy war".'

'I have not seen any, but I understand that leaflets have been dropped by the R.A.F. or distributed by a secret press. These take the form of a Union Jack with a "V" entwined.'

Some acts of defiance were unpremediated as this small incident shows, but gave a great deal of satisfaction nevertheless:

'The Germans once came to search the house to see what they could find. One of them noticed a Union jack over the mirror. He said, "Patriotic, eh?" Without thinking I answered, "Yes, and it stays there until it can go outside".'

The Nightmare

Much of the time most Germans may have shown their best side to Islanders but, as soldiers of the Third Reich, they were nevertheless bound by the Nazi belief in German supremacy and had to obey the harsh dictates of their fanatical Führer. In following these beliefs and obeying these commands, the German authorities in Jersey, as elsewhere, caused cruel suffering and, in extreme cases, death. The innocent victims here were civilians, foreign workers and Russian prisoners of war. Tactics ranged from harassment to wholesale deportations.

Remembering Hitler's anti-semitic paranoia, it is not surprising to learn that the Island's Jewish population were early on singled out for unwelcome attention, though this did not go to the fatal lengths it did in Occupied Europe. From 21st October, 1940, all Jews, or descendants of Jews had to register. By 9th May, 1941, six orders had already been registered against them. The seventh, registered

German anti-semitism displayed in a St Helier shop owned by Jews

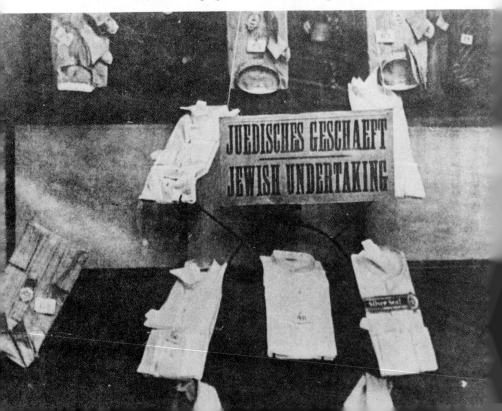

that day at the Royal Court, stated that persons deemed to be Jews could be dismissed from their employment without compensation.

One Jewish business in La Motte Street that had borne the name of 'Moses' before the Occupation, painted out the name before the Germans arrived.

More surprisingly the Free Masons, the Oddfellows and the Salvation Army became suspect. Free Mason Lodges were searched and regalia confiscated.

In January, 1943, Mr Bernard Baker noted, 'Yesterday the Masons, Oddfellows, Buffaloes and similar orders have been instructed to send in a list of all their members'. The Salvation Army was banned from holding open air meetings.

When it came to ordinary civilians, so grossly did the Germans over react to the petty infringements of the ceaseless flood of rules and regulations from the Commandant, that there was actually a waiting list for those who had been sentenced to imprisonment. The prison in Gloucester Street was divided between the Germans and the Jersey prison warders. A prisoner usually went to the German side, often for later deportation to France, if the sentence was a long one. Conditions on the Jersey side were not too harsh. There was even a radio in the prison at one stage and news would also be smuggled in the food that family and friends were allowed to bring in. On the German side, there could be a knock across the head with a luger pistol or solitary confinement. Even if imprisonment was not the outcome for every suspected case of disrespect for the Occupying Forces, the treatment of so called offenders was often needlessly brusque and inhumane. This typical case was reported in November 1940:

'A young woman I know stopped two Germans in a car last week as they were driving up the avenue leading to their farm and told them it was a private road and in any case it was silly to go any further as it narrowed and there were blackberry bushes on each side which would scratch the car. She was told there were no private roads and tho' only in apron and slippers, no hat or coat, was ordered into the car, not allowed to inform her husband nor get hat or shoes and taken to Victoria College House. She was placed in a room by herself for some time and was then taken into another room and made to sit facing three officers with a light shining right in her face so that officers were in the shadow. She was asked if she had ever been in prison and had to give the names of her parents and grandparents as well as those of her husband. Finally she was let off to find her way to La Moye as best she could. She managed to get a cab and arrived back just before 8 o'clock curfew. Her husband all this time had no idea where she had disappeared, she had been gone about three hours.'

Foreign slave workers

To this day there are still some Jersey families deeply scarred by the Occupation, as Senator Dick Shenton recently explained in an interview with Phil Falle, in the *Jersey Evening Post*:

'While others may be making plans to "celebrate" the Liberation, the memory of those days brings back pain to me, and I know it does to many other families.'

'A brother and a sister died during the Occupation and the Liberation saw another sister in Overdale.

Our mother's death followed shortly after and it was obviously connected with what happened during the war. My father was jailed by the Gestapo – thank goodness that was late in the Occupation, otherwise he might not have survived it.'

More widespread in its cruelty was the German treatment meted out to the foreign 'slave' workers and Russian prisoners of war. The first foreigners to arrive came from Spain, to be followed by political prisoners from Poland and Czechoslovakia, together with Jews from Alsace. These, with Russian POW's, whom the Germans contemptuously called untermenschen (undermen), were set to work by Dr Todt's engineers on such major projects as coastal fortifications and the Underground Hospital in St. Peter.

Altogether there were some four to five thousand of these wretches – living in rags and at starvation level – in Jersey between 1941 and 1944. Many are the tales of the pity that Islanders felt for these victims of Hitler's aggression and their attempts, despite their own privations, to help them.

February 1942. 'Spanish workers brought over here were promised better living conditions, plenty of work, good wages and good food and, as they are anti-Franco merchants, a free-pardon after the war. Poor devils, the only thing they'll get will be plenty of work, for their living conditions are very bad and the food barely enough to keep them from starving, about ⅓ pound bread and 1 pint of vegetable stew per day.'

'I found a foreign worker in the alley near us. He said, "Madame j'ai faim". I gave him some bread. My neighbour seeing what I was doing said, "You're not giving him all that!" I told her that his hunger would never be satisfied by just one piece of bread!'

Saturday, 15th August 1942. 'One thousand Russians arrived here yesterday and this morning E. saw about 700 more coming up the pier. These included women and children absolutely in rags and some with nothing on their feet at all. Whatever do they want to bring them to this small place for? I was told that they had been five weeks on the way. Poor souls, one feels so sorry for them. Father saw some being driven in a lorry, he said they were lying on the floor looking absolutely exhausted and just in rags. We used to see this sort of thing at the Cinema, we never dreamt we would see it here.'

'One night we were going to go out of the farm to see the old boy down the road when we saw someone lurking near the door. It was a Russian. He was very thin and he begged for something to drink. So I gave him some milk. He cleared the whole jug. Then we heard the whistle going from Melville House which meant that the Germans had discovered that one of their Russian POW's had escaped. I said to my brother. "Let's shove him somewhere". So we hunged him in a horse box. Then the Germans came and asked if we had seen anybody. When we said "no" they mooched about and then they disappeared. But my brother and I decided it wasn't safe to keep the Russian, so I went to him and said, "You can't stay here". Then I went with him to the quarry and pointed out an old shed where he could hide for the night. I never saw him again.'

Sunday, 30th August 1942. 'One keeps on hearing awful tales of how the Russian prisoners are being treated. They don't know they are on an Island and try to escape, go to the various farms to try to get a little food and the Germans search for them with bloodhounds. These awful tales make me feel ill. I am glad I haven't seen any of these poor souls. I am told that when they landed, the local people had a job to keep their hands off the Germans. There are a lot of them at St. Brelade's and the residents sent a petition to the Commandant protesting against the way the prisoners were being treated. They were told that if they attempted to interfere the Bay would be closed to local people.'

'I saw about 200 Russians being brought along the Esplanade. They were very weak. Men, women and children were walking past the abattoir being taken off towards Corbiere. There were Organisation Todt men with leather whips to keep them moving. They were carrying very few bits and pieces, just bundles under their arms. I saw them being whipped.'

'Some people, when they saw these poor workers, would walk as close to them as possible and drop a crust of bread. They dared not stop.'

'I used to play chess quite a lot. For several weeks I used to play every Tuesday. During 1943–1944 I knew a Russian called George who also played chess with us. He was in hiding from the Germans and being sheltered by some friends of mine.'

'Feodor Polycarpovitch Burriy was an officer in the Soviet Air Force and was shot down near Smolensk in 1942. He was captured, escaped, was recaptured and eventually brought to Jersey after a harrowing journey across Europe. He was in a camp at the foot of Jubilee Hill at Val de la Mare and was abominably treated like everyone else there. He escaped from a work party at L'Etacq Quarries and was first sheltered by Mr René Le Mottée at Millais before being "adopted" by Mrs Louisa Gould, a widow, also of Millais. Mrs Gould was one of a remarkable family as her sister and brother-in-law, Ivy and the late Arthur Forster, also sheltered a Russian escapee as did her sister-in-law and brother, Phyllis and the late Harold Le Druillenec; in fact, they had two!

They were all arrested in the early summer of 1944. Mrs Gould eventually died in the concentration camp at Ravensbrück, Mr Le Druillenec was the sole British survivor at Belsen and Mrs Forster spent the remainder of the war in prison in Jersey.

Feodor Burriy, who had assumed the name of Bill Le Breuilly, was then sheltered briefly, in turn, by Mr "Bill" Williams of Roseville Street and the late Mrs Dorothy Huelin of Trinity Hill, before moving in with two young men, Mike Frowd and René Franoux, who shared a flat on the top floor of No. 7 The Terrace, Grosvenor Street and there he remained until the Liberation.'

Only a month later and Islanders' sympathy and indignation were being evoked on behalf of another innocent group.

'On Tuesday afternoon when the *Evening Post* came out, an absolute bombshell fell in our midst. The following notice appeared:

By order of higher authorities (Hitler himself it is said) the following British subjects will be evacuated and transferred to Germany.

(a) Persons who have their permanent residence not on the Channel Islands, for instance those who have been caught here by outbreak of war.

(b) All those men not born on the Channel Islands and between 16 to 70 years of age who belong to the English people, together with their families.

That same evening Germans started going round warning the people to pack a suitcase as they were to leave at 4 o'clock next afternoon. Can you

Waiting at the Terminus Building, St Helier, to be deported to Germany,
September 1942

imagine how awful it all was? We thought the evacuation of June, 1940
was bad enough but it was nothing compared to this. Then everybody who
left was going to their own country, to speak their own language and live
among their own people, but this was just awful.'

'I was in Millbrooke Park with my little girl and my sister-in-law when a
lady ran up to us with the *Evening Post*. Her face was as white as a sheet
as she showed us the headline. I was English and so was my sister-in-
law's husband. So we both rushed home in a fearful state.'

Wednesday, 16th September. 'They have lost no time in calling up the
people, as they have sent the Constables with a German soldier late last
night waking up people to be ready to go this afternoon. We are all very
distressed and hate them even more for their inhuman actions. Vera
Whiting, her husband, and little girl have gone today. In town people
were in groups, some crying, and some nearly crazy with anxiety
especially as all the families of Englishmen, including the children, have
to go.'

Miss Croad's brother witnessed the first sailing when five hundred
or so gathered at South Hill to wish their departing friends well:

'The boats went out to the sound of cheering from the shore while those
being deported sang "God Save the King" and "There'll always be an
England".'

At the Terminus Building, St Helier, where even stretcher-borne British residents had to wait their turn to be deported

Thursday, 17th September. 'A day of worry for everyone this evening – quite a lot of people that I know have been notified to be ready for tomorrow afternoon. We have heard that yesterday's crowd that went had hot milk, bread and jam sandwiches given them on the pier by the States. They had been ordered to take two days rations with them, but alas our rations are so small that with large families, the rations go as soon as they are in the home.

Friday, 18th September. 'Went to town and observed a very distressing sight of people making their way down to the pier carrying what luggage they can, including a blanket. They were given a good send off by a crowd of people that cheered them from Library Place, as the roads nearer the pier were barred off and had German guards. But they must have seen the unbroken British spirit in that pilgrimage to the boat.'

Miss Croad herself was involved in that Friday's deportations:

'This morning I went across to see Mrs Wilkinson to see if there was anything I could do for her. A pathetic sight to see a mother surrounded by her four children and their luggage on the eve of their forcible transportation to an enemy country. I just wept. The only thing she was needing were some enamel mugs for the children, she was afraid china cups would get broken. I scoured the town, but in vain. Elsie came in and she told me that she had some if I could come out and fetch them. I dashed out on my bicycle to Grouville at 2 o'clock as the Wilkinsons had to leave at 4 o'clock. I got back soon after 3 o'clock and took them in. I found two of their friends saying good-bye and everybody was in tears. The Catholic priest arrived (they were R.C.'s) so I came away and said good-bye just as they left the door. Mr Wilkinson said "Well, here goes the Wilkinson contingent" and they set off down the street each with their blanket and suitcase and wearing as many clothes as possible.

All the afternoon groups of people with luggage in prams, on bicycles and in carts were passing, and it was we who were remaining behind who looked the saddest, nearly all seemed able to raise a smile. Those from the country were brought in buses and a crowd collected opposite the British Hotel to watch them go by. As each bus passed, the occupants were cheered loudly and were answered back by the passengers who were guarded by Germans. One boat was filled and moved off into the roads, but the passengers for the next boat were kept hanging about until nearly 9 o'clock when they were told that embarkation was put off for a week owing to the accommodation being unfit for women and children, which statement nobody believes. The wildest rumours are running round but the general opinion is that something has really happened. The first we knew of it was when we saw people coming up Colomberie with their luggage. I stopped one man and asked him what had happened and he said that one boat had gone but that all the rest had been sent home for a week, but he thought that no more would be heard of evacuation. Time alone will show whether he is right or wrong. Soon the Wilkinsons came in sight, tired out but happy and everybody was shaking hands with them, patting them on the back and congratulating them. On the way back from the pier there were cheers and cries of Churchill, so what the Germans really think of the British, goodness only knows, but they did not attempt to interfere.'

Michael Ginns was one of those deported with his family:

'I went to town with my mother, I was 14 at the time, to see an eye specialist and we were going past the *Evening Post* when I met a friend of my mother's who was coming in the opposite direction and looked as if she had been hit over the head with a mallet. She broke the news to us. The very next day the first batch of people went. The batch I went with didn't go till the Friday so we did have some time to sort out our affairs. Still it was a nasty shock. The day of deportation came. From the various parish halls buses left for town. So we were fortunate in that we were able to get a bus to St. Helier with our luggage. We had one suitcase each. We got down to the railway terminus at the Weighbridge and we sat and waited. All the heads of families had to report to a German typist. If he could speak English, well and good, if not, he had one with him who could speak English who read our details off our identity cards.

My father, who had a heart condition, fainted and the German doctor said, "Bring him round and get him on the boat". So that was that. Soldiers with fixed bayonets lined the route to the harbour. When we got down to the Albert Pier, the St. John's Ambulance and the States had got together to provide us with a bar of chocolate and fifty cigarettes for every man. Richard Mayne, who was then 12 years old, heard about this chocolate being distributed down at the Pier and decided he'd go down with his friends the Matthews to help them carry their cases. He got his chocolate alright but then found himself being propelled up the gangway. He had great difficulty getting ashore again, but he did.

When we got down there the ship was called *La Force*. It was a tender, rather like *La Duchesse de Normandie* that used to run between the Islands some years ago. It was decided there were enough people on it, so one officer got up on a bollard and shouted "Everyone will go to zee ozzer ship". So we went to the "ozzer" ship and it was the *Robert Miller* which had been carrying coal. Dr Sharon, who was the Red Cross and St. John's Ambulance representative said, "You can't put people in that thing" and the Germans agreed. So the officer got back on the bollard and said "Everyone will go back to zee first ship." So we went back to "zee first ship" and we were actually on the last bus load that was accepted down there. They didn't take any more. They said everyone could go home after that. And so a couple of hundred people went home and a lot of them had a nasty shock because when they got home they found that the people who had cheerfully waved them "bye bye" a few hours before had been in and stripped their houses. Not in every case but certainly it happened. I know of a family of a mother and father and five or six children who went home to a bare house, nothing. And it wasn't the Germans – it was the people who were living round about.'

Those people who were turned back went down about eighteen days later and those who were wise hung back and the same thing

British-born residents waiting to be deported to Germany, September 1942

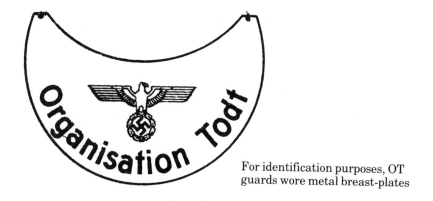

For identification purposes, OT guards wore metal breast-plates

happened again. They were told that was the end of the deportations.

'My in-laws went down to the harbour twice. The second time the man in front of them was told to hold back because of all the children he had. He signalled with his hand for my parents-in-law to hold back too, and they did. In the end the boats went without them and they all came back home.'

This deportation of English families began on 16th September and the third and last batch went on 29th September. Altogether 1,186 people, whose only crime was that they were not Jersey born, were sent to Germany.

The reason for the deportation orders, given directly by Hitler, were said to be in retaliation for the internment of all Germans when British forces entered Iran at the end of 1941. Nevertheless, many of the Germans who had to carry out the retaliatory order expressed their sympathy for those so devastatingly affected by it.

'One day I suppose those of us who survive will look back on it all as if it had been a dream, but at present it is more of a nightmare.'

Friends of the Third Reich

'Jerry bags', the Jersey girls who went out with German soldiers were one group whom the Germans thought of as 'friends of the Third Reich'. Whatever scorn and contempt the rest of the population might have had for them, it was wiser not to show it openly.

'Because one or two of the girl assistants in Boots were suspected of going out with German soldiers, someone once put "Boots for Bags" on the door of the shop.'

Anyone who dismissed a girl from work for being too friendly with the enemy, would soon be asked to re-engage her.

Another group who might also be described as 'friends of the Third Reich' were those Jersey men and women who informed on their neighbours. Yet even some of the Germans were themselves sickened by the stream of anonymous letters that arrived daily in the Commandant's office in College House.

So concerned were a group of Post Office sorters who handled this despicable mail, that they decided to do something to lessen the power of the informers. They arranged to steam open the letters addressed to the Commandant, warn those who had been informed against, and then delay the arrival of the mail for 24 hours. This gave time for the illegal wireless, or bag of corn, or whatever, to be got rid of before the search began.

Did Jersey informers believe that in pointing out individual acts of defiance to the German authorities they were defending the innocent majority against acts of reprisal? Or was the information passed for their own gain? Whatever the motive, sometimes the result was a fine or imprisonment but others informed against ended up in Germany – in one of Hitler's death camps.

To this day much bitterness is felt against those who betrayed, wittingly or unwittingly, their own countrymen and caused them to be sent to concentration camps or to their deaths. Altogether sixteen Islanders died in concentration camps.

Three survivors who were deported on information given against them are John Moignard, Vivienne Mylne and Harold Le Druillenec. In the case of John Moignard's six months imprisonment in France, he says it came about by accident.

Before the Occupation Mr Moignard had been in the motor repair trade but once all private cars were ordered off the roads, he turned his hand to repairing or making anything. His skill was such that he could fashion trailers to hitch behind bicycles, turn biscuit tins into milk cans and repair shoes with old tyres. He even, when fuel became very scarce, converted haulage lorries to run on charcoal. Then in 1942 came his prize invention:

'I built a beautiful windmill to charge batteries. I had wires everywhere supplying neighbours with light. I also made wireless sets, battery powered. One of the people I had working for me was a kid from school. He used to drink cider in one of the pubs in the north of the Island where the Jerries used to go. One day after he'd had much too much cider to drink he started to boast, "We've bombed Berlin. Berlin's blown up." When he was asked, "How do you know that?" he told about listening to the radio at work. Next day three Gestapo arrived. "You the chief of the garage?" Then they questioned me about my wireless sets. But I said, "No I've got no wireless set working here." They searched, they found wireless parts, but they didn't find one working wireless set. It was hidden behind the clock. But I was still given 6 months imprisonment for repairing wireless sets without a licence. I said, "I can't go to prison, I've got eighteen staff working with me." They said, "We'll give you plenty of time to organise your staff." I didn't hear anything for 6 months and then my mother told me, "The Constable's been down. You've got to report tomorrow at 7.0 o'clock. I've got your case packed." Next morning I rang the bell at Newgate Street and then I was deported to France where I spent most of my six months deportation at Troyes.'

In 1942 Vivienne Mylne was a pupil teacher at Jersey College for Girls. She was walking down Roseville Street on her way home from school when a neighbour whispered, 'The Germans are in your house'. Someone had apparently written an anonymous letter to the authorities to tell them that the Mylnes were in illegal possession of a wireless set:

'There were two Germans there and I was taken into the sitting room for questioning. They had already searched the house and they had found the wireless set. They wanted to know the names of the people whom we had supplied with news bulletins. They were fairly menacing but naturally we could not supply them with any names at all. One would never have divulged anything. They took me to prison that night but left my parents at home. I was interrogated every day but it would be incorrect to say that I was bullied. It was just unpleasant and eventually I was told that we would all be tried.

After the trial my father was convicted of having a radio and he was sentenced to one year's imprisonment. My mother was convicted of having withheld information about having a radio in the house and she too was sentenced to a year in prison. I was sentenced to a three year term of imprisonment for publishing the news but the Court recommended mercy and it was reduced to a one year prison sentence. We all went to the old prison in Newgate Street and I can recall that although there was a segregation of the men and women prisoners sometimes the warder forgot to close the gates and my parents did occasionally meet. After a short time

I was transferred to a French prison but my parents were left in Jersey because of their age.'

The most dreaded destination for deportees was Germany. That was where a neighbour's information sent Mr Le Druillenec and his sister. He told his story, as the only British survivor of Belsen, to Betty Brooke, nine months before his death in February 1985, in an *Islander* interview:

'I was involved with my sister who had sheltered an escaped Russian prisoner. My sister, Mrs Gould, had lost one of her sons in England and she was glad to have the opportunity of helping another young man who had escaped from the work camp here. We called him Bill, the Russian whom she harboured, and when someone informed on her, she managed to get him away, but she was tried and so were the rest of the family.

My other sister was not sent to Germany because of ill-health, but we were arrested and sent to Germany. My sister was put to death in Ravensbruck. People often say she died in Ravensbruck, but that is inaccurate. The gas chambers accounted for millions, and even Kramer at his trial admitted that he could scarcely bear to watch the women through the spy holes struggling as the gas rose in the chamber. That is how my sister died.'

Mr Le Druillenec's eight months in concentration camps was spent moving from one to the other. First Rennes, then Belfort and from there to the large camp at Nuemganne. A time at Wilhemshaven followed that and finally he was sent to Belsen.

'I was only nine days at Belsen but the average length of life in Belsen was under nine days.'

When Mr Le Druillenec was released on 16th April, 1945, he weighed only five stone.

One of the most tragic cases of deportation happened just four days before D day. Mrs Bullen begins the tale, which is then continued in the word's of the man's widow in an interview she gave in 1946.

'The day began for me with the startling news that a German who was friendly with a lot of people round about had shot another German last night and was at large and was being searched for, so this morning I had the Germans searching our house and I was also cross questioned by German officers in the afternoon. Olive was in the most trouble, as the soldier went there quite a lot. He was different to the rest and was quite pro-British and hated being in the German Army. He hoped some day to go and live in England or back in Jersey. He was at large for a few days before being captured, and had taken off his uniform to put on civilian clothing. He is probably going to be shot, not only for the shooting but also as a deserter. We all feel very sorry for him though I have not spoken to him.'

'We knew the German N.C.O.,' said Mrs Olive Meurs. 'Though he was a German he was one of the nicest fellows one could wish to meet; there was nothing in the acquaintanceship, he used to come to our house. One day he had been depressed for some time, and told us he had shot his officer. He asked us for food and clothing and said he was going to commit suicide. We refused to give him clothes at first as we did not want to be involved, but, finally, to save a scene in the yard, we gave him some old overalls and jacket which we used for fishing, and he went off. He still had his revolver with him and we thought he was going to shoot himself, but he did not and was caught. That same night the German police were after us; they searched the house, knowing that he came there, but found nothing, but after a time they came back and told us they knew very well we had assisted him and that it was a serious crime. My husband was taken away and placed in prison, where I was allowed to see him every Saturday and take him food, but on the fourth Saturday, when I went I was told he had been taken away the previous night. He was asleep, they woke him up, gave him ten minutes to dress and took him to a ship which was leaving for France. Others who went with him were told some time before that they were going and were allowed to take extra food and clothing, but poor Edward was given no such consideration and he went without even an overcoat.'

Nothing further was heard of Edward Meurs until a Monsieur Florin from Switzerland appealed for the relatives of an Edward Meurs who had died at Liegenheim, near Cassel.

One touching aspect of the whole nightmare of deportations is the supporting link that was sustained through the Red Cross, between those who had been carted away from Jersey and those who were left. Mr Stanhope Landick remembers how one of the teachers from the Intermediate School did not forget her former colleagues even in her own dire straits. Miss Margaret Barker was deported to Biberach internment camp with her parents and brother. From there, in 1943, she managed to send a Red Cross parcel with chocolates and cigarettes to be shared among the staff.

D-Day and After

After the rout of Dunkirk four years earlier, D-day brought British troops back to France once more. Both the Occupiers and the Occupied in Jersey had known that the invasion was imminent. When and where were the imponderables. The Germans thought mid-June and they considered the unlikeliest spot the west coast of the Cotentin – the impregnable fortress of the Channel Isles would have to be attacked first.

Islanders hearing of the air raids on Alderney and Guernsey knew something was up. When, on the night of 5th June, they heard wave after wave of aircraft pass overhead, rumour was rife. In Guernsey they believed that all the Germans in Jersey were ready for instant evacuation – so that they would not be cut off from their troops on the Continent. Jersey believed that the States of Guernsey had offered £25,000 for the Occupying forces to leave their Island. Both firmly believed that Normandy had been chosen for the invasion so that once it fell the British troops could turn round, as it were, and liberate the Channel Islands.

At daybreak on 6th June, Colonel Heine, however, sent a messenger to Coutanche with a proclamation to quell any misguided patriotism. This urged Islanders to keep calm and warned them to refrain from acts of sabotage. Any attacks against German forces would be punishable by death. That same day the Germans took over one of the Islanders' last symbols of freedom – the telephone exchanges.

No proclamation with its death threat, no German controlled telephones, however, could suppress the great joy that the British invasion of France had at last happened and that better times were just one step ahead.

6th June, 1944. 'In two days Rome had fallen and the invasion begun. What a night we had last night. The excitement started soon after 1 a.m. I was awakened by the drone of 'planes which went on and on and on. Off went the guns all over the place, the noise was deafening. As soon as the guns stopped for a while, the fun began. I could hear the Germans being knocked up, banging on doors and shouting, for there were many billetted nearby, and soon there was as much traffic about the streets as if it were midday. The guns started up again at about 5.30 – I have never heard such a rumpus – and again at 6.15 and 8 o'clock. As we live in Colomberie, we are quite close to the Fort. None of us had been able to sleep with all this going on, and when my father went down about 6 a.m. to open the shutters a man passing said that they had all been sent back from the

Left: Blampied's cartoon
illustrates the following
poem, written by Winter Le
Brocq in June, 1944.

'Inditement'

Rumours of Carteret taken
And Coutances . . .
Of splendid death
Of swift and violent
*   carnage . . .*
But in the markets
We,
With anger on our lips,
Cry at the price of
*   strawberries.*

quay because it was the invasion. How I longed for my wireless. The telephone was cut off but the news spread like fire round the Island and we were all wildly excited.'

Gradually the euphoria of D-day evaporated. The Islanders' fond hopes of an early liberation were replaced by the chilling realisation that every invasion success in France meant more, not less, hardship. For though appeals were made to Hitler by his own Generals to release the vast number of troops tied up in defending the Channel Islands, the Führer was adamant. Eleven days after D-day, Hitler went further – he ordered that the Channel Isles and Cherbourg had to be defended to the last.

The more entrenched the Germans became in Jersey and as more wounded Germans were evacuated here from mainland France, the more mouths there were to feed. To ease the situation somewhat the slave labourers were deported back to the continent. This, though, was not enough.

1st to 20th August. 'We are now getting completely cut off from France and dependant on our own resources, but we don't mind going a bit short, as long as it won't be long. Our rations have been cut down further lately. Bread, adults 4½ pounds, chicken 3 pounds, 5 pounds potatoes, 7 ounces breakfast meal, 2 ounces butter, 1 ounce salt, 3 ounces sugar (child 6 ounces), milk ½ pint adults, children 1 pint. Some weeks 8 ounces macaroni. But in spite of our difficulties we are all very cheerful and grateful for the real news that leaks through, for our *Evening Post* is a pack of lies which of course is partly under German control.'

As one by one the French Channel ports fell, the Channel Isles were in a position of siege, cut off from all supplies from France and forced to subsist on what they alone could grow.

Once the Allies had liberated France and their thrust to reach Germany was irreversible, there were nevertheless some advantages for all Channel Islanders. In Jersey illicit wirelesses could now be tuned to the BBC Forces network. Best of all, the fall of France opened up a short escape route for young Jerseymen eager to help in the Allied war effort. Out of the fifty nine who attempted the escape, forty seven were successful – many helped to sail from Fauvic beach by William Bertram and his family:

'My eldest brother went with two others in two rowing boats in 1945 and landed at Carteret. He left a note with someone to give my mother the next day. He didn't tell a soul he was going. He was scared to. "We'd have known if he hadn't made it and the weather was good," mother said, then "No wonder he was always out and round La Rocque." Later on we got a Red Cross message to say that he was O.K.'

Peter Crill, Roy Mourant and John Floyd were a trio the Bertrams helped. Their daring plan took nearly two months to put into effect. First they borrowed a removal van to take Mr Crill's twelve-foot dinghy *Alouette* from a store in St. Helier to a shed in St. Clement. They bought the engine for the boat from a Gorey fisherman, the petrol they stole from a German store.

They managed to obtain a weather forecast from a German meteorological officer, and knowledge of when German guards patrolled Grouville's coast road. Then with rope and a small quantity of food, they finally set off on their journey to France from Fauvic between eight and ten on the 11th November.

After rowing for an hour, they started the engine but it broke down and they drifted helplessly all night. Fortunately, though, they were being blown by a constant north east wind. 'It was all very British. We got there in the end,' was Mr Crill's comment. For at daybreak they saw the light of Le Sénéquet light house. After their seventeen hour ordeal on meagre Occupation rations 'we were pretty well at the end of our tether', remembered Mr Mourant.

They eventually landed just north of the Le Sénéquet lighthouse on a deserted beach near Geffosses. John Floyd stayed with the boat while the other two, who could speak French, went off to find assistance. They were warmly welcomed by the French and once they got back to England, Peter Crill went to Oxford, Roy Mourant joined the Navy and John Floyd the Army.

Nevertheless, these two advantages did nothing to alleviate the desperate straits in which both Occupiers and Occupied now found themselves. So impenetrable was the British blockade of the Channel Islands, that if troops and civilians were to survive – the British would have to be asked to lift the blockade.

Churchill's reply on 27th September, 1944, was adamant. 'I am entirely opposed to our sending any rations to the Channel Islands ostensibly for the civil population, but in fact, enabling the German garrison to prolong their resistance.' But there were 28,500 troops and 62,000 civilians on the islands to be fed and only food enough to last until January. Medicine, soap, cereals, sugar, salt and tobacco were immediately needed.

It is ironic, therefore, that the longed-for event by the Channel Islanders, the invasion of France by the Allies on June 6, 1944, should have had such dire results. Their position was not bettered after the landing on the Normandy beaches. Instead, they were reduced to conditions they had not had to endure in all their previous four years of Occupation – conditions of great privation and of near starvation.

V for Vega

There was only one move left after Churchill's refusal to lift the British blockade that was starving Occupier and Occupied alike. That was to ask the British Government's permission to approach the Red Cross. Already escapees to England from Guernsey and Jersey had given graphic accounts of the plight in which Channel Islanders now found themselves. The following report from four Jerseymen was printed in *The Times* as early as October 1944.

'The food situation in Jersey is getting acute. There are about 16,000 German troops in the island. They have sufficient food, they say, to last them until January 31st, and they plan to fight until then. There are 40,000 civilians in Jersey and they have only enough food to last them until the middle of next month. The 30,000 civilians in Guernsey are even worse off for food. It is hard to see how our people will manage. There is now no sea communication with the Channel Islands, and if any food was sent to the civil population the Germans would get it. By the end of the present month civilian medical supplies in Jersey will be exhausted; there will, for instance, be no anaesthetics left. The Germans have sent a lot of their wounded to Jersey, and they, too, appear to be short of medical supplies as they are using paper bandages in their military hospital.

The health of our people remains fairly good, but among children there is consumption and rickets due to malnutrition.'

In November 1944, therefore, the two Bailiffs were at last allowed to appeal for aid to the General Secretary of the International Red Cross in Geneva.

'After what seemed like years, we were told that a relief ship carrying supplies of "prison of war parcels" and other essentials was to be sent to the islands from Lisbon. Hopes went up high and then gradually dropped again as the days went by, the supplies petered out one after the other. Larders became quite empty and then just before Christmas we received news that the International Red Cross Ship *Vega* was expected to leave Lisbon within a few days for the islands. It eventually arrived in Jersey about 6 p.m. on January 1, 1945 having called and discharged part of her cargo at Guernsey first. It was more than a thrill to see that ship steam through the pierheads with all her lights ablaze. The first friendly ship we had seen in 4½ years. Hundreds of people went to all available vantage points to gaze on the ship which meant so much to us. The next day unloading was started, the actual unloading being done by German troops. St. John's Ambulance men acted as the civilian guards and guarded the parcels day and night, until each civilian had received his or her parcel safe in their own custody. The ship brought enough parcels to allow two for every man, woman and child, in addition a number of invalid parcels, salt (2 ounces per head), tobacco and cigarettes. The tobacco was

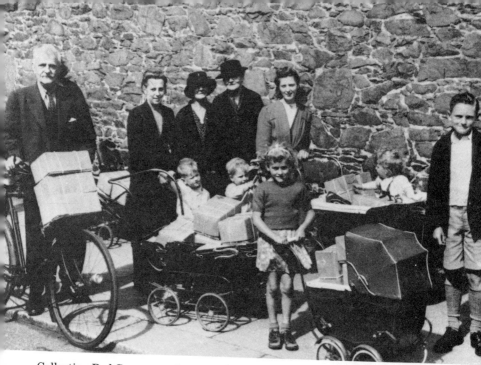

Collecting Red Cross parcels in whatever containers were available

insufficient for a ration, (cigarettes 10 each to every man and woman) and 150 layettes – the gift of Lady Campbell's fund, the wife of the British Ambassador to Portugal. We received our parcels on January 2nd, 5th, and 6th. They consisted of a 10 pound (approx) cardboard box of foodstuffs made up as follows: 1 tin kam (pork), 1 tin sardines, 1 tin corned beef, 1 tin Klim (powdered milk), 4 ounces tea, 6 ounces sugar, 1 ounce salt and pepper, 1 carton biscuits, 1 tin (pound) butter, 1 tin (pound) jam or marmalade, 1 carton raisins, 1 carton prunes, 1 tablet chocolate, 1 tin salmon and in some boxes, coffee was substituted for tea. One other commodity the ship brought was soap and this was issued at the ratio of 1 tablet per household. Now imagine if you can the thrill this parcel gave to the majority of us who had not seen the majority of the contents for over four years. It has made all the difference to our lives since we received them. The second parcel (the same contents as the first) was issued on February 6th and a third issue, the first of the second consignment is expected next Tuesday, February 20th. The parcels are, up to now, the gift of the Canadian Red Cross for Jersey and the New Zealand Red Cross for Guernsey.'

The effect of the food parcels on both Islanders and the Germans ranged from self indulgence to self restraint. One man ate so much of his parcel at one fell swoop that he had to be rushed to hospital. The

The Swedish ship *Vega* gave sustenance and hope to Islanders long deprived of 'luxuries' such as tinned meat and chocolate. Reproduced by courtesy of the Jersey Museum

Germans, however, despite being so near to starvation themselves, never once attempted to divert the food parcels from the civilian population.

'I can remember going to collect my Red Cross Parcel from the shop at the end of the lane. There was great excitement. The best thing after the *Vega's* visit was the white bread; to taste that again after that mucky stuff with husks was such a treat. To go and get white bread was like a teenager of today going to buy his first computer.'

'My father and elder brother went to collect our food parcels. They had a horse and cart to bring it all home. You didn't even touch your parcel straightaway. It was like a Christmas present. The first thing I took out to eat was the chocolate – I hadn't seen chocolate since 1940.'

'The Red Cross parcels contained food the existence of which we'd almost forgotten. Tins of fruit and all manner of good things which we appreciated very much indeed.'

'There was real tea inside the parcels and after all the years of dried blackberry leaves and other substitutes we wanted a cup of real tea as much as anything.'

'That line from the 23rd Psalm – "Thou preparedst a table before me in the presence of mine enemies" – it didn't mean much to me in earlier days. Now it means that just at the time when we'd been three weeks without bread, suddenly, out in St. Aubin's Bay, appeared the Red Cross Ship *Vega* loaded with the Red Cross parcels and real flour. That first piece of bread we had some days later, that first bit of bread, was better than any

New border to the Occupation-carved 'Vega + 1945' in the Royal Square, unveiled by HRH The Duchess of Kent in 1985

cake we'd had before, absolutely incredible. To suddenly have some real white flour bread after 3 weeks of no bread at all, was a revelation.'

1st January, 1945. 'We salute the New Year, not with a heavy heart, although our cupboards are bare but with the joy that the Red Cross has fulfilled her promise to the friend in need. Our hearts go out in gratitude and thank God for his mercies. May this year bring an end to this war; peace and reunion with our loved ones we all pray.'

March 1945. 'On Friday we were glad to welcome the *Vega* here with her cargo of flour, parcels etc. which was most welcome. They were very quick at unloading and we had some lovely white bread on the next Tuesday. It is impossible for those who have always had their daily bread to realize the appreciation which was manifested with the distribution of our lovely white bread, for it is cake in comparison to the bread we have had for years of occupation. Our ration is 4 pounds adults, children 3 pounds. Our food parcels have also saved us from starvation for if it was not for the great help of the Red Cross we would have practically nothing. No bread, butter, sugar, salt, potatoes, and milk only 4 days weekly, ½ pint per day. The Germans have wanted us to go without milk altogether, but the officials have fought hard to keep it. They are in a very bad way for food.

The soldiers haven't much strength in them and are fed up. There have been two acts of sabotage by the troops. One at the Palace Hotel which has been gutted and a garage in New St. John's Road.'

It is no wonder then that there were many manifestations of the gratitude that Islanders felt not only for the *Vega's* first visit, but for the supplies it brought on subsequent visits. Not only was a special Thanksgiving Service held on 7th January but the *Evening Post* started a fund for the Red Cross in recognition of the relief they had brought. Over £1,000 was donated in just 24 hours. By the end of the month the grand total was £25,000.

April 1945. 'The Island is working hard to get money for the Red Cross Fund. Concerts, sales, raffles, and in all sorts of ways we are trying to bring in a big sum. La Rocque chapel had a Thanksgiving Service and the retiring collection realised £56. Mrs Dodsley has a light entertainment in Miss Le Vesconte's tea room and is raising a big sum. We are all strung up with the good news of fighting in Germany.'

In appreciation of the Swedish ship, one baby was even christened Vega. Even more permanently, underneath the very nose of the Germans, was set in stone in the Royal Square – VEGA + 1945.

Our Dear Channel Islands

'We thought we were going to be blown to pieces rather than surrender – some of the Germans were real fanatics.'

May 1945. 'We know now that the end is near. On Friday 4th we had great excitement with news that the Germans were to capitulate on the 5th but our hopes were damped down as it was a rumour.'

5th May. 'The town is like a fair this morning, everybody buying flags and red, white and blue decorations.'

Sunday, 6th May. 'A little more excitement today for we are aware that the end is near and the air is full of tension and rumours.'

Monday, 7th May. 'We are in great excitement for we know now that any day we shall be relieved. During the evening we dug up John's wireless which has been in the ground for two years. Having kept it for one year in the house, and as things were getting hot for me, I had to decide on this action.'

7th May. 'Everybody seems to think that the troops will come tomorrow. The political prisoners were set free this evening, and the Americans are to be freed tomorrow.'

Tuesday, 8th May 1945. 'Truly this is the greatest day of our lives for most of us in these islands. Wireless sets sprung up from everywhere and we heard Mr Churchill's speech. Our emotions were overwhelmed when he mentioned the dear Channel Islands would be freed today. After the speech (just after 3 p.m.) all put their Union Jacks up and other flags of the Allies. Anyone who has not had the experience that we have had under occupation can not realize what it meant to hoist our beloved flag once again. For five years we have had our patriotism suppressed. We could only show our faith in the future by our acts and forbearance. This evening I walked to town and back with some friends. We expected the fleet to arrive today but were disappointed, but we enjoyed ourselves immensely and thought it wonderful to be free and without 10 o'clock curfew. We arrived home about 11.30 p.m. It was wonderful to see the electric on once again and no blackouts!'

'Suddenly I heard there was something going to happen in the Royal Square. I thought I'd go along to find out. I found the Square absolutely crowded with people. Walking along behind just outside was a German soldier with his gun slung over his shoulder. He didn't know what was going on and neither did I. But I saw that up in the trees there had been some very large loudspeakers installed. Suddenly there was Alexander Moncrieff Coutanche on the balcony over the States building announcing that shortly there would be a broadcast. Sure enough at about 3 o'clock the loud speakers cracked into life and there was the voice of Sir Winston Churchill coming over saying, "The war in Europe ends today and later today our dear Channel Islands . . ." – "hurrah" roared the crowd. I never heard what he said about "the dear Channel Islands".'

8th May. 'What a day! Every time we listened in we heard that this was Victory Day – and here we were with nothing different. And then the news spread that Mr Churchill's speech was to be relayed in Royal Square, Howard Davis Park, and the Parade, after which we could hoist our flags. Then about 1 o'clock the *Evening Post* came out with all details and uncensored news, so then we began to feel quite different. The Square was full of people all wearing red, white and blue rosettes. There was an absolute silence when Mr Churchill began his speech. When he spoke of the "dear Channel Islands" there was a loud cheer. As he finished the Union jack was hoisted on the Court on the Club, together with the Jersey flag, and I can't tell you how we felt. Then the Bailiff made his speech and told us that a British naval force was on the way, at which the cheers were deafening, that there was no longer any ban on wireless sets (more cheers) and that all prisoners would be freed tomorrow. After which we sang "God save the King". The *Vega* was just coming in on a beautiful high tide, but it was the Navy we hoped to see. It is an awful funny situation today. Here we are all free, but so were the Germans. We went to hear the King's speech and took our bottle of champagne with us, also saved for five years.'

'Just before the Liberation we were getting a bit careless and had attached our crystal set to a gramophone amplifier. We heard Churchill

British Naval officers mobbed as they come ashore

The defeated German troops waiting to be embarked for the U.K.

loud and clear. When he spoke of "our dear Channel Islands" we broke into tears.'

'The Commandant of the Channel Islands was stationed in Guernsey. As the British ships approached to relieve the Channel Islands, he said, "No the war in Europe comes to an end today at midnight, and if you approach before midnight then we fire". So the British ships held back and that is why everyone talks of VE day as 8th May but for us Liberation Day was 9th May.'

Wednesday, 9th May. 'I left at 1.30 p.m. with the children in a little handcart en route for town. We went to the end of Victoria pier and there saw some Germans packing up. What a glorious sight for us who have been under their domination for so long. We waited a long time expecting some of our Tommies to land. For there were some big ships just outside in the roads. Little boats were sailing up and down and we had the joy of seeing our Jack Tars. They had a great reception. We were just making off for home when someone called out there was a boat coming in. We raced along to the middle pier to welcome them. What a reception! They were simply mobbed and could hardly move. We heard there were some Jersey men on board, so all who had their loved ones in the forces were eagerly looking if they could spot one.

I saw a touching scene of a mother who found her son. We all cried. It was a touching episode. We had a good time shaking hands with the soldiers and cheering. We could hardly move with the crowd. Eventually we arrived back home past 11 p.m. very tired.'

'I can remember my sister and I being taken to the foot of Mount Bingham. There were all the boats coming in and out of the harbour all day and there was the sight and sound of all those Bedford Army lorries coming up Mount Bingham one after the other. All the lorries and the uniforms of the Tommies seemed brand new after what we'd been used to. The Tommies would occasionally stop and hand out cigarettes and chewing gum – I'd never seen chewing gum before and we'd take a bit out and pass it along for someone else to chew. Everyone was so happy.'

9th May. 'Had a service at the church at 11 o'clock. Meanwhile there was great excitement on the piers, for a destroyer was sighted at about 10 o'clock coming around Noirmont Point, and when the landing party came ashore they were mobbed. Finally two officers were carried shoulder high to the Weighbridge. At about 1.30 the first planes roared overhead and everybody waved frantically. Tonight, when the soldiers came ashore, they were mobbed as well. It was a perfect evening, and what with the destroyer, the *Vega* and the calm sea, and St Aubin's Bay looking so lovely, and everybody walking so happy, one felt one must be dreaming.'

12th May. 'The BBC tonight called it the most momentous day in the history of the Channel Islands, and it is right. Colonel Robinson had asked for it to be made a public holiday. This evening at 6 o'clock there was the Proclamation in the Square. It was very thrilling to hear the King's

German guns thrown over the cliffs by the British after the Liberation

message. It was worth while going through the last five years to live the last five days.'

The following extract is from R. C. F. Maugham's book, *Jersey Under the Jackboot:*

Nobody living in Jersey will ever forget that wonderful 9th May. On that historic day the people saw at last the men who had become to them almost beings of fable. St. Helier gave itself up to celebrations such as the Island had never before witnessed. Every man, woman and child became a centre of whole-hearted joy to themselves as well as an unending fountain of adulation to their deliverers. Countless voices sang and shrilled, a swirling sea of exultancy swelled and swept madly, rising to mighty waves of acclaim. Before, beside and behind the incoming warriors, the crowds pushed and struggled and fought for a handshake, heedless of the motor traffic which at times threatened life and limb. As new arrivals made their appearance, the crowds rushed to greet them, drunk with the ecstasy of their newly-regained freedom, great eddies in a vast, irresistible whirling tide of joy. These were not only our liberators, they were the Men of Marathon who had won what may well prove to have been civilisation's final battle; men of great armies to whom the shadow of swift-moving doom gave but increased power and tenacity such as inspired the host of Cyrus and Cambyses. They were, in a word, men of our own blood and king, the soldiers of Britain. Small wonder, then, that we lost our heads; this day, of all the days in her history, was Jersey's Great Day.

BUCKINGHAM PALACE

To my most loyal people in the Channel Islands, I send my heartfelt greetings.

Ever since my armed forces had to be withdrawn, you have, I know, looked forward with the same confidence as I have to the time of deliverance. We have never been divided in spirit. Our hopes and fears, anxieties and determination have been the same, and we have been bound together by an unshakable conviction that the day would come when the Islands, the oldest possession of the Crown, would be liberated from enemy occupation. That day has now come and, with all my Peoples, I cordially welcome you on your restoration to freedom and to your rightful place with the free nations of the world.

Channel Islanders in their thousands are fighting in my service for the cause of civilisation with their traditional loyalty, courage and devotion. Their task is not yet ended; but for you a new task begins at once – to re-build the fortunes of your beautiful Islands in anticipation of reunion with relatives, friends and neighbours who have been parted from you by the circumstances of war. In this task you can count on the fullest support of my Government.

It is my desire that your ancient privileges and institutions should be maintained and that you should resume as soon as possible your accustomed system of government. Meantime, the immediate situation requries that responsibility for the safety of the Islands and the well-being of the inhabitants should rest upon the Commander of the Armed Forces stationed in the Islands. I feel confident that the Civil Authorities, who have carried so heavy a burden during the past years, will gladly co-operate with him in maintaining good government and securing the distribution of the supplies which he is bringing with him.

It is my earnest hope that the Islands, reinstated in their ancestral relationship to the Crown, will soon regain their former happiness and prosperity,

(Signed) GEORGE R. I.

The King's Message to the Channel Islanders